I'm Dying
Shit! Not Again!

♥○♥

*The story of one woman's
three near death experiences,
her spiritual unfolding and her
urgent message to the world*

by

Cha~zay Ph.D., C.H.

Publisher

This book has been published in collaboration with Create Space and Dr. Cha~zay and is also available in eBook format through her website at the following address:

http://www.corefreedom.com/resources/book-im-dying-shit-not-again.8/

It is also available through Amazon Kindle and Smashwords.

New Versions

The urgency of the release of this book did not allow for any delays needed to professionally edit this book, which would have only delayed the release of this urgent information. Visions are constantly being added to this book and new version are coming out periodically. Below is the current version available. To register for our newsletter so we can keep you posted on new versions and new books coming out by Dr. Cha~zay, please send a blank eMail to 3nde@aweber.com.

Current Version: 3
Last Update: May 5, 2013
ISBN Number-13: 978-1484897300
ISBN Number-10: 1484897307

Legal Disclaimer

The author is not a licensed medical practitioner, medical doctor, psychiatrist or psycho-therapist. She is an Metaphysician, certified Hypnotist, Reiki Master and Certified Grief and Suicide Hotline Counselor. If you are concerned about your own or anyone else's mental stability, please consult a professional. If you are suicidal,

call 1-800-SUICIDE (within the United States). If you are elsewhere, please reach out to someone. Everything in this book reflects the author's personal journey as a woman, and reflect her own vision, experiences and her research into this topic through the interaction with her clients.

Rights and Copyright

Contact

Telephone U.S.: **901.800.9696**
Media/Radio/Speaking: media@corefreedom.com
Community: www.CoreFreedom.com
Consulting: www.Cha-zay.com
Facebook: www.Facebook.com/drchazay
YouTube: www.youtube.com/BlueprintForLove
Mailing List: 3nde@aweber.com

♥☺♥

Dedication

This book is lovingly dedicated to the eternal magnificence of you, the reader.

♥◊♥

Special Thanks

You would not hold this book in your hands if it wasn't for my loving parents who took on a great assignment in teaching me so many beautiful life lessons.

A special thank you goes to Oprah, from whom I learned speaking English, unbeknownst to her, when I first arrived in the U.S., speaking no English.

A few years ago I was called to Vancouver to participate in the *"I Can Do It"* event where the following people spoke:

- ♥ Louise Hay
- ♥ Wayne Dyer
- ♥ Marianne Williamson
- ♥ Carolyn Myss
- ♥ Cheryl Richardson

The messages each and everyone of you imparted were significant and life changing as it was during this conference that I was told to write this book. I hesitated and procrastinated and returned to the school of hard-knocks for a few years - and yet here it is. Thank you all for your magnificence and living your calling so that people like me can step up to our own brilliance too.

To all my friends who know me so well, to whom I come for safety, shelter, feedback and advice, your guidance has been invaluable, impeccable and without this book wouldn't exist.

May Source richly bless all of you!

Subliminal Messages

This book has been sprinkled throughout with subliminal messages to help you remember your magnificence.

Your conscious mind does not need to be able to read these messages. It is your Subconscious' job to pick up the messages from each page.

If you do not resonate with any of the following messages, which are printed invisibly on every page, either refrain from reading this book or take out a ruler and pen and cross out what does not resonate with you, while telling yourself that you are not accepting a specific affirmation.

I AM LOVE • YOU ARE LOVE • YOU ARE BLESSED • YOU ARE A BLESSING TO THE WORLD • YOU ARE ALL KNOWING • YOU ARE ALL PERMEATING • OMNISCIENT • OMNIPRESENT • WE ARE ALL ONE • YOU EXCUDE HAPPINESS • YOUR BELIEFS BENEFIT YOU AT ALL TIMES • YOU ARE ALWAYS AT THE RIGHT PLACE AT THE RIGHT TIME • YOU ARE A BLESSING TO THOSE AROUND YOU • YOU ARE DISCERNING • YOU ARE FILLED WITH WISDOM • YOU ARE A BEAUTIFUL SPIRIT EMANATING ONLY WHAT IS LOVE • YOU ARE HEALED AND YOU ARE A HEALING INSTRUMENT TO ALL THOSE AROUND YOU • PEOPLE AND LIFE EVERYWHERE LOVE BEING IN YOUR PRESENCE • YOU ARE LOVED • YOU ARE DIVINELY PROTECTED AND GUIDED • YOU ARE ALWAYS IN THE RIGHT PLACE AT THE RIGHT TIME • YOU ARE HEALTHY IN MIND, BODY AND SPIRIT • YOU ARE CONFIDENT • YOUR SELF ESTEEM IS HIGH • YOU ARE FOREVER EXPANDING IN SPIRITUAL KNOWLEDGE • YOU ARE TRANSCENDING PETY THINGS • YOU ARE GIVING AND YOU EASILY AND HAPPILY RECEIVE • YOU ARE A GREAT COMMUNICATOR • YOUR FRIENDS ARE FILLED WITH INTEGRITY AS ARE YOU • YOU ARE SURROUNDED BY A DIVINE SUPPORT SYSTEM • YOU LOVE YOURSELF AND THEREFORE HONOR YOUR BODY TEMPLE • YOUR SOULS

EXPANSION IS OF UTMOST IMPORTANCE TO YOU • YOUR FELLOW TRAVELERS' SOULS EXPANSION IS OF UTMOST IMPORTANCE TO YOU • YOU ARE KIND TO ALL BEINGS • YOU ONLY SPEAK WHAT IS BENEFICIAL IN LIFTING UP EVERYONE, INCLUDING YOURSELF

♥O♥O♥O♥O♥O♥O♥O♥O♥O♥O♥O♥O♥O♥O♥O♥O♥O♥O♥O♥O♥O♥O♥O♥O♥O♥O♥O♥O♥O♥O♥O♥

Table of Contents

About the Author..18
Introduction - Message from the Author 20
  Grammatical Errors and Typos................................. 20
  An Urgent Message 20
  I'm Not Your Guru - You Are.....................................22
Religious Comments 24
  Nuggets of Wisdom...24
  Premonitions and Intuitive Work............................25
Chapter 1...27
Do You Ever Feel Like You're Death Is Near? 28
Chapter 2 33
Early Childhood 34
  Four Forms of Punishments 35
  There is a Witch in the Forest................................ 36
  Running Away at Three 36
Chapter 3 39
First Near Death Experience 40
  Paths of the Forest 41
  The Forest of Life 44
  I'm Gonna Marry a Farmer 44
Chapter 4.. 47
Imbalance In Our World 48
  Disconnecting From Life.. 48
  An Astrological Beating 50
  My Soul Is Disconnecting 51
  'Psychiatrists Need Psychiatrists'............................52
  A Butterfly's Broken Wings 52
  My Exit Strategy..53
  Your Life Line on Paper 54
  A Clean Slate 56
Chapter 5 57

An Experience To Die For 58

Chapter 6 63

Urgent Information About Suicide 64

    Death by Overdose: 64

    Death by Aspirin: 64

    Death by Tylenol: 64

    Jumping off the Golden Gate Bridge: 65

    Pulling the Trigger: 65

  A Few Facts About Suicide 66

  Common Misconceptions about Suicide 66

Chapter 7 69

Second Near Death Experience 70

  Back In the Body 76

  The Love of Source 78

  Back Home 79

  A Knock on the Door 80

Chapter 8 83

Life Continues and Turns 'Normal' 84

  Moving Out At Fifteen 84

  I Want To Live! 86

  Forgiveness 87

  Life's Hurdles 88

  Heeding Spirit's Interference 89

Chapter 9 91

My Third Near Death Experience 92

  Being In Touch With Your Mortality 95

  Stop Chasing The Skirts, Drugs and Other Nonsense 95

  The Light That You Are 96

  Allow Your Soul To Speak and Expand 97

Chapter 10 99

Major Decisions 100

  Marriage and Family 100

  Impacting Time and Space 102

Chapter 11 103

Reading People's Thoughts 104
   Be Careful What You Ask For 105
   Learning How To Read the Universe's 'Thoughts' ...107
   Learning To 'See' 108
   Ghost Dividing Itself 109
   Everyone Is a Teacher.......................................110
Chapter 12.. 111
Dying Again 112
   The Real Tragedy of Divorce 116
Chapter 13.. 119
Giving Life Over to Source................................120
   The Biggest Decision of My Life.........................121
   WARNING!.. 122
   Finally - She's Ready!.....................................123
Chapter 14 125
Which Side Is Talking?.....................................126
Chapter 15..129
Karma versus Cause and Effect............................130
Chapter 16 133
My New Assignments - My New Life 134
   Celibacy..134
   Groups, Tribes and Reading Books.........................137
   Partnering With Your Divine Partner.....................140
   My Next Assignment - Living Without Food 141
Again!? 144
Earth Changes 149
Chapter 17...151
The Fabric of Our Soul 152
Chapter 18 157
The Four Doors of Life 158
Chapter 19 163
Ask And You Shall Receive 164
   The Day You Die 165
Chapter 20...167

Time Line 168
   1971: First Near Death Experience (5) 168
   1971: Spiritual Experience (5)................................168
   1973: Felt Called To Vegetarianism (7) 168
   1978: Lost Interest in Life (12) 169
   1981: Second Near Death Experience (15) 169
   1984: Decided to Live (18) 169
   1989: Moved to the United States (23)................169
   1991: Third Near Death Experience (25)................170
   1993: Birth of our Daughter (27) 170
   1996: Lymphoma (30)......................................170
   2000: Spiritual Unfolding Continues (34)............171
   2004: Separation from Husband (38)................171
   2005: Lemurians 171
   2006: Giving Over Life......................................171
   2007: Dying Again 172
   2008: Looking For Aneurism 172
   2008-2009: 'Get Out'......................................173
   2010: Moving to Italy.....................................173
   2011: Moving to Switzerland............................173
   February 2012: Moving Back to the U.S. 175
   May 2012: Moved to Sedona, Arizona..................175
   August 2012: Last Meal 175
   September 2012: Barefoot Hiking 176
   October 2012: No Water 176
   December 21, 2012:..177
   2013: 177
   2013 - 2017:...180
   2017 - 2022:...184
   2022-2023:...184
   2023-2027:...185
   2027-2029:...185
   2029-2052:...185
Chapter 21..189

What You Can Do 190
   Your Future Higher Self 191
   Getting Your Life Together 191
   Changing Your Story...................................192
   Forgiveness 194
   Facing And Mastering Fear 196
   Powerful Mantras 197
   Meditation and Nature 198
   The Power of Water....................................199
   Get Support and Become Your Own Guru 201
   Self Care...202
   Finding Freedom At Your Core.................... 203

Chapter 22 205

Summary 206

Miscellaneous and Resources 207

Speaking and Appearances 232

Core Freedom - A Life Skills Community...................... 208

Teleseminars by Dr. Cha~zay.............................. 212

Other Books by Cha~zay 213

Twin Flame Forum and Dating 217

Study-at-Home Courses by Cha~zay 219

Get Unshakeable Confidence and Self Esteem.............224

Free Teleseminar Training Course 226

Anatomy of a Goal 227

Donations 231

Resources 233

Notes 234

About The Author

♥○♥

"There is nothing as important as the evolution and expansion of your soul."

Cha~zay, Ph.D., C.H.

About the Author

Cha~zay lived through three near-death experiences and three near fatal diagnosis. Although living on both sides of life and death for decades, she spent the first part of her career living in the business world before starting her own consulting company in 2003.

Cha~zay, Ph.D., C.H

She was a Learning Annex and Learning Exchange facilitator for many years and has spoken on stage with Robert Kiyosaki (author of Rich Dad Poor Dad).

When tragedy struck in 2006 she lost nearly everything, including her health, her business, and all of her assets. She was guided to leave the business world and truly embark on her spiritual journey. Guided into solitude and detached from most of society she has spent the last seven years in the Italian and Swiss Alps getting taught and re-aquainted by Nature and her own guru within. Mid 2012 she was urged to move to the United States to assist with the 'rebuilding' process by coming forward with her life purpose.

Today Dr. Cha~zay is a Metaphysician, certified Hypnotist, Reiki Master, published author, speaker and workshop leader. She is considered a spiritual mentor by many of her community members; she leads an online life skills community where topics of love, relationships, spirituality, and topics related to the

unseen world are discussed with members from all corners of the world. She has become a beacon of hope to the hopeless.

She is the creator of four powerful web widgets that contain the same basic energy patterns the Universe uses to unfold and refold matter: cleansing and creating, transmuting and transforming. Over fifty five thousand of these widgets are appearing on websites and blogs around the globe.

She holds a customer service degree from the government of Switzerland, a Ph.D. in Metaphysical Science and a Ph.D. in Holistic Life Coaching. She is also a Reiki Master, certified hypnotist, suicide hotline counselor and non-denominational ordained minister.

Dr. Cha~zay speaks seven languages including sign language. Her favorite language, however, is the language of energy - of unconditional love. She believes that if love is all we are and love is all we sow, then love is all that can grow.

Her International client base include individuals and businesses from countries such as the U.S., Italy, Switzerland and various other European countries, Australia, India, Ukraine, Malaysia, India, Russia, the Philippines and many others.

Today Dr. Cha~zay spends most of her time teaching others how to bring their own magnificent and unique and authentic message to the world by means of teleseminars, reaching the globe and people everywhere.

♥0♥0♥0♥0♥0♥0♥0♥0♥0♥0♥0♥0♥0♥0♥0♥0♥0♥0♥0♥0♥0♥0♥0♥0♥0♥0♥0♥0♥0♥0♥0♥0♥

Introduction - Message from the Author

Grammatical Errors and Typos

The urgency for this book to get into every man, woman and teenager's hands at this present moment in time, demanded that this book to be written in a two day period and there simply wasn't enough time to edit it and make it grammatically perfect or free of typos. In fact, English is my fifth language, you are bound to come across grammatical errors and typos. It is my hope that you forgive such little details and instead can focus on the urgency of the message.

An Urgent Message

The utmost urgent time has come for this message to be distributed to the world. Not in a few months from now or next year - **NOW**. This is why there is no price tag attached to the e-version of this book but offered in exchange for donations (unless you bought it through Amazon or Smashwords). This book must be in everyone's hands. I urge you to spread the word, you will shortly see why.

Not only is humanity hurting, our planet is hurting as well as our furry, feathery and scaly fellow travelers - all beings who are trying to experience their life here in this dimension. We are all being squeezed through the birth canal of this Universe and the contractions are intensifying for everyone. Birth must be given. The question is - what will be born?

As Buddha so eloquently said: *"The trouble is you think you have time."*

We don't have time. Time has already run out for many. Don't let it run out for you.

The rubber band has been stretched to its limit and is either near its breaking point or is about to snap back, causing upheaval humanity must be prepared for.

Perhaps this message can wake up as many as possible. For the rest of you who do not get this message, don't despair. Know that eternity is a long time - that's how long we have to do this again and again. My question to you is, why repeat the same class over and over again? Don't we graduate from pre-school in order to go to Kindergarten, and then move on to primary school, high school and eventually enroll in college and grad school? Why enroll in the school of hard-knocks and repeat the same semester over and over again? Isn't that the definition of insanity?

Please know that once upon a time I not only repeated many semesters in this school of hard-knocks, I eventually got so good at repeating the same mistakes over and over again, that I was offered the position of dean at this world famous school. I accepted the offer when later I realized that I should just own the darn thing. Of course, I'm being cynical.

What I am saying is that I am the queen of banging my head against the same wall over and over again, simply not getting the messages, or perhaps I didn't want to get them. What else can you call three near death experiences and three near-fatal diagnosis than getting hit over the head by our loving Source of all that is, and with all this still not getting the message?

I finally got it! And I'm typing 90 words per minute trying to give you the nuggets my life has been putting through the fire again and again to get the diamonds I can hopefully bestow upon you through these lines.

I'm Not Your Guru - You Are

Nothing is more revealing than when people are looking for their spiritual master or guru, rather than looking for their own inner guru. If you get only one thing out of this book then it is this - **you must find your own inner guru**. That's what this entire book is about. YOU must find your own internal truth. Always remember that no one can teach you anything that you don't already know. So everyone, including me, are only here to help remove obstacles that prevent you from seeing that you are your own magnificent guru. Truth is already there, all you need to do is allow for it to percolate into your conscience.

Bruce Lee said it so well: *"A teacher is never a giver of truth, he is a guide, a pointer to the truth that each student must find for himself."*

And Khalil Gibran said that *"The teacher who is indeed wise does not bid you to enter the house of his wisdom but rather leads you to the threshold of your mind."*

In other words, I can't teach you anything. No matter what you learn here, you are still left to your own devices in testing out for yourself what has taken me decades to learn. You must find your own truth as well. So do your own work, don't take my word for it. In fact, I urge you to question everything and everyone, including everything in this book.

We are living in a world that teaches children how to assemble numbers, and put together vowels and consonants into words, but we fail to teach our children how to think. As a result our graduating population is getting better and better at regurgitating unimportant information while the world lacks to produce geniuses. Most of humanity are completely incapable of thinking for themselves. It's time to wake up. NOW.

Thomas Watson Sr. said it best: *"THINK."*

So please, by all means, utilize this most precious gift of thinking and then make appropriate choices.

♥0♥0♥0♥0♥0♥0♥0♥0♥0♥0♥0♥0♥0♥0♥0♥0♥0♥0♥0♥0♥0♥0♥0♥0♥0♥0♥0♥0♥0♥

Religious Comments

Please know that I am not affiliated or associated with any specific religions nor do I participate in any particular religious practices. Having just one near death experience ought to wipe out any religious tendencies in anyone, drawing them forever closer to the incomprehendable Source of all that is. As a Metaphysician and woman who has 'seen' and experienced the 'other side' more than once, I will do my best to explain to you what 'God' is and what 'God' is not. Remember that it is impossible to ever explain God with 26 vowels and consonants. God can never be understood but can be known, no words are needed. In fact, words distort the very image of what God is.

The Dalai Lama explained true religion best: *"This is my simple religion. There is no need for temples, no need for complicated philosophy. Our own brain, our own heart is our temple, the philosophy is kindness."*

I find my religion of kindness and gentleness easiest to access in the silence and solitude of my inner sanctuary. Nature has become my church.

Nuggets of Wisdom

Take what resonates with you but do not ever take this or any other writings from anyone, ever, as the 'holy grail' of all that exists. There is no such book or one person who has all of the Truth and nothing but the Truth. The Truth (capital 'T') remains with Source. And we are Source, each of us have our own interpretation of what Truth is. It is this interpretation then that create each of our truths. Our truth, however, is always based on

biases, experiences and worst of all, our beliefs. I will talk more about our belief system in a later chapter.

What is important for you to remember is to question everything I say in this book. Not as in doubting it, but as in truly inquiring within your own Self. The big Truth is within you and only you. And you have access to that Truth by going within, by finding your own inner guru within you, because that is where the only reality exists.

I can only share with you my experiences and my journeys, I can share with you what happened to me and how I *reacted* and *acted* based on these experiences. I can share with you my thinking processes and tell you about the choices I made. But I can't give you the Truth, this is something you will have to get for yourself by going within. And perhaps my sharing my truth will assist some of you to draw closer to your own Truth within.

So remember the Zen proverb: *"Teachers open the door, but you must enter by yourself."*

Premonitions and Intuitive Work

While my friends call me a closet-psychic I will deny to the end of my days that I am psychic. I don't like the term, not because I don't believe in psychic people, I do, but because the word has been abused so much (from both sides), that the vibration of the word itself has turned negative and is therefore non-beneficial. Therefore, I will refrain from giving detailed premonitions, I will especially withhold exact dates and exact locations, and will keep things open so you can inquire within yourself. There are a few things that I will share and it is of utmost importance that you do not take my visions at face value because not only do they

change constantly, but that you go within and weigh your own truth there.

Because of the urgency of what is taking place 'behind the scenes' it is of utmost importance, however, to get this book out into the world NOW. I will sprinkle in between these lines messages, which will be heard by those who have inner ears and can see with inner eyes. To those of you who do not have well trained inner ears and inner eyes, I urge you to train them now! How? You must silence your mind and retreat to the garden of Eden within where all treasures lie. You will find this garden of Eden by going into silence and solitude. Make Nature your church. At minimum retreat within the sanctity of your own mind during meditation. This is a **must** and there cannot be any excuses not to find this inner peace at this time.

Time is running out...

♥0♥0♥0♥0♥0♥0♥0♥0♥0♥0♥0♥0♥0♥0♥0♥0♥0♥0♥0♥0♥0♥0♥0♥0♥0♥0♥0♥0♥0♥0♥0♥0♥

Chapter 1

Death is Near

♥○♥

"Enlightenment is the complete eradication of everything we imagined to be true."

Adyashanti

Do You Ever Feel Like You're Death Is Near?

The following is a post I placed in our forum. You can read the post with all of its comments by clicking here:

http://www.corefreedom.com/threads/do-you-ever-feel-like-youre-death-is-near.1221/

"I want to speak to our family members here in the community. You've known me for a while and I've been quite open and transparent about my life. You know that I've had three near-death experiences at the ages of 5, 15, and 25. I have spoken about my second near-death experience here in this forum. And I've been under doctor's supervision for three near-fatal diagnosis since then. Obviously, death is not scary to me and I constantly walk in the awareness of my body's mortality. And you also know that I live on the 'other side' (if there were such a thing) more than I do on this side.

"Ever since I was a little girl I was given a powerful vision of a woman who was 50 years old. This unknown woman, only visible to my inner eyes, had been my role model growing up and carried me through some tough times in life. Only recently have I recognized that this woman was a premonition of my Self in the near future. A few years ago I was given a premonition of a most important date, January 18, 2052, at which point I would be 85 years old.

"And yet, recently I've been receiving other visions when receiving visions of the one I love so endlessly, the one that feels like the Self I am. And in those visions he looks solid and yet I am spirit. I don't feel 'dead' but I clearly look like a spirit. Add to this that I've been

urged to stay away from the cost for the past few years and suddenly Spirit's guidance has been clear for me to move to Los Angeles (of all places). My most recent vision was being in an earthquake, although I can't see the end of the earthquake. Now all my visions of the future are just Polaroid pictures of movies that once played in my inner eye.

"In all these years Spirit has surprised me again and again by showing me that just when I think I know how something works - everything changes. And I realize over and over again that I really know very little, if anything at all. Letting go of what I think I know has been a blessing in disguise because I have ceased to be surprised. And I have found an endless fountain of peace this way.

"And yet here I am getting recurring thoughts to cross my Ts and dot my Is, meaning that I need to inform my closets friends and family members what to do, what I 'have' (bank accounts, passwords and all this bureaucratic hoopla stuff). There is a sense and urgency of writing letters to people. I keep my life pretty up to date and clear of unresolved issues and as of this moment there is no one I need to mend any relationships with or apologize to or ask forgiveness for - because I do this on a weekly, monthly and yearly basis. I strongly believe in living a non-attached life, free of burdens and hooks, whether they are emotional, energetic or tangible.

"I took this picture a while back holding myself in the palms of my hands. This was going to be the front cover of my book where I talk about my life journey, dying, living, dying again. And now I no longer feel the need to publish the book. Now I just feel like being in a state of love at all times. Sometimes I feel like I'm bursting with the love I feel. And often this body feels too tight, too much of a burden to contain all that is. And I can't even say where this energy is coming from. It's not from a man, not from my child, not from our puppy. It's pure Source energy - and it bursts forth from within.

"So whether physical death is imminent is not important. If today was my last day and I had to ask myself if I have loved enough, I could say 'yes.' If I asked myself if I have forgiven enough, I could say 'yes.' If I asked myself if there was any unfinished business here for me to do, frankly I would have to say 'no.' I love in the endless moments of eternity and my moments are filled with so much bliss that it doesn't matter if I have one more moment left or a billion more moments in this body temple. My state of bliss is permanent and surpasses this vessel.

"Would love to hear from you - if you've been feeling similar things in the past, or perhaps now. Sending you all love and bliss!"

Cha~zay, Ph.D., C.H.

♥O♥O♥O♥O♥O♥O♥O♥O♥O♥O♥O♥O♥O♥O♥O♥O♥O♥O♥O♥O♥O♥O♥O♥O♥O♥O♥O♥O♥O♥O♥O♥

I placed the above entry in our spiritual community and the response within the community and behind the scenes has been overwhelming. If you would like to read the entire thread with people's responses, you can do so here:

http://www.corefreedom.com/threads/do-you-ever-feel-like-youre-death-is-near.1221/

The number of people that contacted me via eMail, Facebook, and by other means, telling me that they have been feeling similar things, has caused me to 'snap out' of whatever stagnant energy I seemed to have been stuck in. In the above thread I talk about not feeling the need to publish the book, and yet since receiving so many overwhelming responses from people who are feeling the same urgency to get their T's crossed and I's dotted, it has become clear that nothing could be more important than to give you this message of urgency.

Buddha says: *"The trouble is you think you have time."*

How right he is!

Leonardo daVinci said: *"I awoke, only to find that the rest of the world is still asleep."*

It is time now for humanity to wake up.

♥0♥0♥0♥0♥0♥0♥0♥0♥0♥0♥0♥0♥0♥0♥0♥0♥0♥0♥0♥0♥0♥0♥0♥0♥0♥0♥0♥0♥0♥

Chapter 2

The Witch in The Forest

♥٥♥

"The usefulness of the cup it its emptiness."

Bruce Lee

Early Childhood

From the very get-go of this human life I struggled not only being healthy, but especially with the want to be on this planet in the first place. Life as a little girl was tough. I was born quite ill, to parents who were heavy smokers. My mother had severe gallbladder problems during her pregnancy with me and surgery was not possible. In the 60s they didn't know any better, and gave my mother regular morphine shots to help ease the pain. I was born with asthma, acute eczema all over my skin and eye and ear distortions. The eczema was so bad that my skin was constantly itching and bleeding. I was put on cortisone cream as an infant and later put on cortisone shots from the ages of 4 to 14. Cortisone by far was the most devastating drug that created all kinds of havoc in my body. By the time I was 12 years old I was disqualified from school sports because I was constantly sick and in physical pain. My body retained an abnormal amount of water and I looked like a plumped turkey. The worst part was the constant physical pain. I would get out of bed walking like an old lady, and that's exactly how I felt. No twelve year old should feel this way but I didn't know any better at that time.

My constant feeling ill caused me to be an angry little girl and as far back as I remember I did not want to be here. I did not deal well with the constant physical pain. I asked my mother one day how come no one asked me if I even wanted to be here. She said that I didn't have a choice and that she and my dad decided to have a child and so I was born. I threw a fit telling her that someone should have at least had the courtesy to ask me because I really hated this life. I was barely four years old.

I used to think that I had a normal family life, but as you will see, and as I became an adult and with hindsight by my side, I admit

that my life was hardly normal. Today I realize that perhaps it was so dysfunctional because 80% of today's families are just as dysfunctional - it helps me relate and understand the basic reality of so many people's upbringing.

Although my mom was a stay-home mom, she always seemed absent, angry at something or someone and disappointed, cynical and critical of seemingly everything and everyone. I could never figure out if her disappointment was with me, with the man she chose or her own choices she made in life. My sister was born a year after me and as a result I was expected to be a good role model to her. Unfortunately for me, I didn't know how to let my anger out on my parents, they just seemed so big and the beatings and punishments were unbearable at times, so I threw a lot of tantrums and fits, which of course resulted in my getting punished even more.

Four Forms of Punishments

We had four forms of punishments. Get hit in the head, usually in the face or the back of the head, sometimes my butt as I walked by, go to bed without dinner, house arrest and room arrest. Usually I endured three of these verdicts at the same time. House arrest meant that I could roam free within the apartment but playing outside was out of the question. Room arrest meant to be locked in my room, usually for the rest of the day, up to a week or two. I could go to school but as soon as I came home I had to be in my room for the rest of the day.

There is a Witch in the Forest

Children don't have a sense of time, which is the way it should be, even for adults we realize that bliss is near when we have no sense of time. As we are trained in learning linear time, we start to put ourselves into the illusionary box of time. I never knew when I would be able to leave the room, if ever, if I would be forgotten or if I would starve to death. I got really good at looking out the window to study the forest nearby. After all, my mother's favorite bedtime story was Haensel and Gretel. She never failed to finish the story with a warning: *"And if you don't behave your Dad and I will one day leave you in the forest too."* What made this so difficult was not only that we lived near the forest, I stared at it every day, but that we went for walks in that same dark forest every Sunday afternoon.

Every week I spent walking on egg shells, never knowing if this Sunday would be the day I was left in the forest for the witch to find me and eat me.

Running Away at Three

Living in such constant fear and lack of safety one day I decided to take matters in my own hands. I took my two year old sister's hand, I was three years old, and told her that our lives were not safe and we needed to flee. Hand in hand we walked for two miles, crossed major intersections and walked along a major road, from our little town to the next big city, where a woman looked out the window and saw two little toddlers walking by themselves. She took us inside her home and started to make phone calls until she found our parents.

I was in room arrest for a long time as a result of running away.

♥0♥0♥0♥0♥0♥0♥0♥0♥0♥0♥0♥0♥0♥0♥0♥0♥0♥0♥0♥0♥0♥0♥0♥0♥0♥0♥0♥0♥0♥0♥0♥

Chapter 3

First Near Death Experience

♥○♥

"When the inward tenderness finds the secret hurt, pain itself will crack the rock and let the soul emerge."

Rumi

First Near Death Experience

One day right after my fifth birthday I was in the bathroom where my mother was blow drying my hair. My sister peaked around the corner in an attempt to tease me. Wanting to run after her but forgetting that my mother was blow drying my hair, my mother grabbed my arm and hit me so hard that I slipped and head first crashed onto the edge of the toilet. I was unconscious immediately and found myself in a most blissful place. It was a place of such peace and such light and love, that I knew I never wanted to leave this place again. This felt so familiar, this is where I wanted to stay, not this earthly place that I disliked so much. I did not float through a tunnel and do not remember seeing life flash before my eyes and I was not welcomed by any relatives and I don't remember hearing any angels sing. I simply found myself in heaven, in pure bliss, a place of golden light that was so surreal that it is nearly impossible to describe.

The next thing I remember is my consciousness coming back to this three dimensional reality where my mother was holding my limp, lifeless body. I was back in my body but unable to move for a few seconds. I heard her say: *"See what you made me do? I didn't mean for this to happen."*

I felt guilty for making her mad, as a child I always felt like I was the reason for her unhappiness and her frustration. But no matter how hard I tried, I never seemed to manage to make her proud of me or love me. I would never hear 'I love you' or sit on her lap. My life as a child consisted of walking on egg shells, never knowing when the next smack in my face would come down on me as they always came without warning. Life consisted of surviving and finding my own inner strength within.

I was finally able to open my eyes and when I saw her panicked look on her face, all I knew was that I was back in this life but I no longer wanted to be here, I wanted to be in this 'other place,' this heavenly, golden place where I had just been.

I asked my mother: *"Am I dead?"*

With panic and irritation she responded: *"Of course you're not dead, what non-sense."*

I disagreed: *"But this life is just a dream and not real, the other place where I just visited is real. How can I get back there?"*

She responded angrily: *"Stop talking such non-sense, we have to go to the hospital."*

I had a major gash on my forehead and needed to get to the emergency room quickly. I suffered a concussion and needed stitches, other than that I was as good as new. At least on the outside.

Paths of the Forest

On the inside, everything changed. And the outer world changed as well. Up until this time I was a rambunctious child, wild and defiant, angry and unable to sit still. Thank goodness spirited children were not put on medication yet back then, or my spirit would have for sure been quenched by drugs and adults who didn't want to deal with me. Instead of retaining my restlessness, I suddenly withdrew. People started to scare me and intimidate me, I felt in the way, out place, like a stranger who just didn't belong on this planet. I became so shy that my mother would introduce me as: *"And this is the shy one."*

Already as a five year old I stopped being a participant in life and simply became an observer. I didn't talk much, people were no longer of interest to me, they simply didn't feel safe. I withdrew from people and retreated to the farm next door where I tended to my chores.

My nights were spent flying away, slipping out of my body and flying over our village, then over our country, then away from the planet into other dimensions. I often asked my parents if I could go to bed around six or seven at night. It served a dual purpose, for one I would prevent getting punished for the rest of the night but most importantly, magic seemed to unfold as the birds started to quiet down, and I felt the need to do the same. Every morning I was up with the birds around five or six, depending on the season. The rhythm of Nature became my way of life and has remained with me for the past five decades.

Even as a child I only drank water from the faucet in spite of being offered bubbled water or fruit juices. Water to me is a holy substance and today I only drink distilled water and do much manifesting with water. Water is the most priceless substance our Mother Earth has to offer, worth more than food.

After this experience my visions changed and the world looked clearer and more vibrant. I started to see energy swirls, funnels and vortexes in the empty space as they were drawing endless symbols. I loved laying in corn fields where no one would see me, looking up at the top of the corn while watching the sunlight dance with these vortexes and funnels. Today I would describe this as the sunlight making love with the sacred geometric symbols that make up this illusionary world. As a child, however, all I saw was a beautiful display of colors and sound waves where others just saw nothing.

I also started to be accompanied by a voice that was neither male nor female. It always said the same thing: *"Never forget that something very special is going to happen to you one day."*

I never asked who the voice was or where it came from, I didn't ask what special thing would happen to me, I simply found comfort in being accompanied by such a heavenly presence.

My fear of the forest still existed but now I was able to turn my fear into courage. Now I became eager to visit the forest every Sunday because I no longer entered the dark woods with anticipation of one day being found and eaten by a witch, now I was entering the forest with the determination to get to know its very inside. I wanted to learn every trail and memorize every tree. I wanted to be prepared if ever I was left there, so that I would be able to find my own way out. Instead of clinging to my dad's pants I now asked to skip ahead and veer off the path. I was convinced that this forest one day would become my home and I was determined to learn and memorize every path.

As a result of my new determination I was ambitious to learn how to read forest maps. Thankfully and coincidentally, although there is no such thing, our main field trips in first and second grade were all about learning how to read forest trails. We were paired up, given a map and sent off into the forest as seven year olds to find our own way through the forest. I excelled at map reading and my sense of direction and acute awareness of the space around me provided to be of huge service to me.

The Forest of Life

Now that I am in my 40s I see life just the same way. Although we are not given a map to get through the forest of life, the ability of reading life's clues and hearing heaven's guidance to assist us in getting to our destination are just the same. All we have to do is know how to read the clues and cues and then take appropriate action.

Just like I could get side tracked in the forest with looking at a pretty tree or getting lost over the little pond over there or losing time watching a family of deer, life has its own distractions too. Most adults are distracted by shiny objects, pinks skirts, TV programs or yet another new gadget that promises to make our life better, richer, more efficient while providing the illusion that the Joneses will for sure be impressed. And when these distractions cause us to veer off our life's purpose for too long, we cause ourselves unnecessary stress by not living our soul's truest purpose. It is important to enjoy the sights and life's beauty, and it is also important not to lose sight of the path that we're on.

I'm Gonna Marry a Farmer

Shortly after this life changing experience I was approaching the farm when suddenly everything in my periphery started to twirl and change into a moving picture. Only the graveled path leading up the farm and going straight through the farm, seemed to be steady and lit up in golden colors. I froze in place when suddenly the right side of the farm was magnified as if someone was holding a huge magnifying glass over the right side of the farm. To the right of the path was the main house, the vegetable and

flower garden, the fruit trees, and the chickens. This was the domain of the farmer's wife.

The magnifying glass moved over to the left side of the farm where there was the building housing the cows, another building housing the pigs, the corn silos, the heavy equipment, and the tractors - this was the place where the men spent their days working.

The path going straight through the farm was lit up with so much golden light that each of the gravel stones looked like diamonds glistening in the sunlight. I intuitively knew that this was my path in life, to build a farm.

In a flash I knew that this little farm not only sustained the farmer's family and employees, but it also provided food for the village. In fact, once a week it was my job to take my red bicycle with the little basket in front and bring the eggs, butter, flowers, fruits and vegetables to the locals in town.

In complete awe of the magical picture unfolding before me suddenly there was an energy enveloping me that felt so much like the voice I had been hearing. Only this time I didn't hear the voice, I felt it. It felt like this place of the golden heaven that I visited, and here it was, enveloping me, hugging me on this graveled path approaching this farm. There was so much love contained within this energy, I was in such bliss, I never wanted to move and just stay there so this bliss would never end.

In an instant I realized that it was my job to marry a farmer!

As an adult of course I realize that this vision has nothing to do with a farm or a farmer husband. It has everything to do with merging masculine with feminine, living a balanced life and only

when we live in balance, first within ourselves, and then within the relationship with the life partner we choose, can we find bliss and peace. And together then can these two people create a purpose that not only benefits them and sustains their life, but their merging benefits humanity as a whole.

Unfortunately the majority of adults do not understand that the ultimate purpose and goal of any partnership is always to serve humanity, most are still reducing their partnership to basic chemistry and their own selfish needs. And as soon as Nature has done her job and chemistry wears off, there is no more purpose for the relationship to be sustained and neither the two people nor the planet gets to benefit. On the contrary, now the two people are in agony or at minimum wasting their lives and in doing so are robbing not only themselves, but they are robbing the planet of the amazing fruits they have truly come to deliver to this planet.

It is time now for humanity to take it up a notch and rise beyond just the first three chakras and the sensed oriented world. It is time now to come into balance by observing what is chemistry and what is higher purpose. Merging the two will allow not only for children to be created who will become socially responsible adults and geniuses the world needs so desperately, but it will help couples create new paradigms and projects that will propel humanity upward and forward into states of peace and love.

♥○♥

Chapter 4

Broken Butterfly Wings

♥〇♥

"All know that the drop merges into the ocean, but few know that the ocean merges into the drop. "

Kabir

Imbalance In Our World

Neither the farmer's wife nor her husband's side was more important to their personal survival or the nourishment and growth of their village. In fact, if the wife did not do her part the farmer and the rest of the workers would have no vegetables, no fruits, no eggs, no butter, no beds to sleep on, no home to call a home. And if the farmer did not do his job, the wife would not have the flower to bake her bread, her corn to cook with, and the cows wouldn't get milked. There would be no sowing and reaping of new crops.

The two are essential to the union and sustainability of the farm. And in knowing their place the village was able to count on them for delivering the foods they needed.

The world as it is today, however, still sees women as *'lower than'* men, *'less important'* and a species to be controlled, manipulated and used. The world as a whole has not yet learned that neither is more important than the other, and that only together can the human race be sustained and happiness, peace and balance be achieved in this world.

Disconnecting From Life

Life became increasingly difficult for me as a child after these events. I wanted to be in this heavenly, golden place and no matter how far and thoroughly I searched the forest, I couldn't seem to find a place here on Earth that looked or felt even remotely like it. Life on the farm was peaceful and I felt safe with the animals, and saddened that pigs and cows that I had felt 'close to' were seemingly disappearing from time to time. Each

cow had her own name and I became intimately familiar with each cow's character and personality. The day came when I realized that the animals were not disappearing but were actually sent to the slaughter house. I was seven when I became a vegetarian.

The funnel, vortexes and swirls were still there, but not as frequently as before. At the same time I became more and more withdrawn as I noticed that I would just 'know' certain things about people. I didn't know how I knew, I just knew. This 'knowing' intensified as I got older and at times it was unbearable. There was absolutely no one to talk to about these things, I knew that no one would understand or even believe me.

When I was twelve years old my Dad left our family and took my sister with him. He didn't say good bye, never said a word, never called again, he just disappeared. From my mother I learned that supposedly he never wanted me anyway and that he claimed in court that the only reason he married my mother was because she was pregnant with me. He apparently accused her of getting pregnant on purpose and told her that if at least I was a boy he could have loved me.

Most of my life I heard that I was in the way, a loser and that I would not amount to anything. I didn't excel in school and was bored out of my mind to learn something I had no interest in learning. My mind was completely shut down to the teachings of the educational system. So much so, that I dropped out of eight grade and moved into a horse back riding stable to embark on a career with horses. I went back to school much later in life when I could study subjects that stirred my heart.

An Astrological Beating

Around this same time one of my mother's friends was studying to become an astrologer. My mother offered my birth data so she could use my information for her studies. My mother gave me the final report for my twelve birthday. All I remember is that the report said that I would always be surrounded by medical doctors due to bad health and that I would have to be careful with drugs, alcohol and sexual activity.

Hold on a second, I was already struggling with life but now there was an actual report that claimed that these flickering dots in our sky were actually making me do certain things and that I had no control over my own life!?

My entire world crumbled at the realization of not having free will and the lack of freedom to make my own choices was simply not going to work for me. I felt like a puppet on a string, with my last piece of freedom robbed and no matter what I chose to do in life, I now was controlled by rocks in the sky. I remember feeling an anger and rebellion in me that I hadn't felt in a long time. In that instant I wanted to show *'the Universe whose boss'* and I decided that I would never smoke, never drink, never do drugs and that I would never have a one-night stand. I became determined that I was to be in control over my life and only I. No stars in the sky and no person on the planet would ever control me.

Today I smile at my 12 year old arrogance, but it worked. I had mustered up enough angry energy in that moment, which I still remember to this day, that the decision became a frame work of how I want to experience life. I realize today with hindsight by my side, that all of life is just a series of choices.

At the end of this chapter there is an exercise for you to do. Don't skip it.

My Soul Is Disconnecting

And yet there I was, realizing at the age of twelve that I was obviously not only an unwanted child, but that my birth seemingly brought so much pain to my parents, I started to dream of getting back to this blissful, golden place in heaven. I started to contemplate suicide.

I asked the voice to stop talking to me, to stop comforting me, I asked it to go away. And it did.

Feeling lonelier than ever, I remember feeling a disconnect from my soul to this physical body. I lost interest in life and was determined to take my own life. If I could only find the right method. I knew I didn't want to experience much physical pain. Jumping off the bridge and having my body splattered all over the road or river bed was not an option. I tried cutting my wrists but that was too painful. Hanging myself seemed too complicated and not practical for where I lived. Getting a firearm was an impossibility and it didn't seem 'final' enough. What if I missed?

All I wanted was to drift off and re-experience the sudden reality of this golden, blissful heaven. And having to suffer to get there wasn't appealing. The mind of a twelve year old can come up with the most illogical thoughts, and sometimes that's a good thing. Or perhaps they were blessings in disguise as my pickiness in how I would end my life was delaying the process. Perhaps some of you can relate.

'Psychiatrists Need Psychiatrists'

Even though I didn't share my deepest, darkest thoughts with anyone, for some reason my mother had the insight to send me to a psychiatrist to make sure I was dealing with the divorce of my parents in a healthy way. As I was sitting in front of this gentleman who was holding up flash cards before me, I remember thinking to myself: *"He needs a psychiatrist."* Why would he keep holding up black and white cards featuring butterflies? It just didn't make sense and such a waste of time.

Every time he held up another card I responded something like this:

"A butterfly with holes in its wings."

"A butterfly getting ready to fly away."

"A butterfly getting ready to land."

"A butter fly with broken wings."

All I saw were butterflies.

A Butterfly's Broken Wings

I refused going back to him and felt it a great waste of my time to look at butterfly pictures. I was not diagnosed with any conditions and it was determined that I should not be on medication. Mentally I seemed to be okay. Emotionally, however, it was clear that I was longing to fly and be free. I was longing for peace and transformation. And yet I felt like my wings and will to live were broken. I had no wings to fly away with.

If I could only die...

After my Dad moved out, I never heard from him again through my teenage years. Never got a phone call or an explanation. He just disappeared. I let out my anger by writing him a letter, telling him that I considered him dead from now on and to never contact me again. It was just as well, he obviously didn't care and with me contemplating ending my life he would not have to hurt and wouldn't miss me a bit, so I thought.

The statistics in the United States confirm that 50% of divorced fathers never see their children again one year after the divorce. If fathers only knew how important they are in their children's lives. If fathers only knew that when sons and daughters are mad at them and never want to see them again, they don't mean it on a soul level. What they say is the exact opposite of what they need. If fathers would only continue sending love, even if it's just a card or a text saying "I just wanted you to know I love you and I'm thinking of you." If fathers only were the adults instead of resolving that they are not needed, no important. If fathers only would put their children before their new girlfriends.

And if mothers would stop emasculating and chasing away the man they once said was the love of their life and would stop tearing down the father of their children, boys and girls would grow up without the dysfunction so prevalent in today's society.

My Exit Strategy

I spent three years, until I was 15 years old, contemplating my exit strategy. It was a lonely three years filled with frustration because I couldn't find an easy way to end my life, and it was depressing because I didn't want to hurt my sister.

What ended up winning me over was the realization that I was just 'in the way' and utterly unwanted. I felt like a burden, not only to both of my parents, but to the planet as a whole. I could see things in people and knew things about people but there was no way I could explain what I saw and knew and therefore I was unable to help. I didn't have the slightest idea of what to do with the information. My body was sick from the cortisone and every day I got out of bed feeling like an old woman with a dying body.

I didn't see the purpose for my life and my feeling homesick to this golden, blissful heavenly place won me over.

Before I go on with my story, let's do an exercise. I created this many years ago and it has helped me hugely in learning how to take better responsibility for the choices in life.

Your Life Line on Paper

Take out a piece of paper. Draw a line down the middle of it. This is your life line. Mark the bottom of the line with 0, this is your moment of birth, and the top of the line with 90 or 100, the end of your life. Then divide the line up according to how old you are today. On the left side you write down all of the things that signified an important <u>positive</u> life changing event for you. On the right side you write down all of the <u>negative</u> events that took place in your life. Write them so that they are on the level of the age at which you had the experience. Rate them on a scale of 1 to 10, with 10 being very blissful or very painful. One would be close to the center line, 10 would be on the outside edges of the paper. Now connect the dots all the way up your life line.

The end result will be a zigzag path of your life all the way to where you are today. You will see that your life has hardly appeared in a straight line.

The next thing you can do is look at each of the events and ask yourself how much of these events were caused or initiated by your own choices, versus which of them were out of your control. My own divorce for example, was as a result of my own choices. My parents divorce, however, was out of my control. As you take review of all of these life changing events you will see that 80-90% of the events in your life occurred as a result of your own choices.

Note: Sometimes people ask me where to put an event that felt really bad at that moment but then turned into a blessing later. Put the event in the column of how you were first impacted, not your later results. So if your husband asked you for a divorce ten years ago and you were devastated, then put that in the "negative events" column. Today, however, you may have found your true love and so in hindsight your divorce from ten years ago was a blessing in disguise. You may be tempted to put this event in the "positive events" column, but for the sake of this exercise use the energy of what it was like at that moment. The purpose of this exercise is to get a real snap shot of what took place in each moment.

As you will look at your life you will see that considering everything it did not take a huge number of events to guide to where you are today. Sometimes just one event can propel us to go into a completely different direction. Just a handful of events over a decade can mold and shape us into the person we are today.

A Clean Slate

The most amazing part of this exercise is the empty space ahead of you. Let's say you have marked the top of the page with 90 as in turning 90 years old, and today you are 45 years old. You have done your exercises and you see the zigzag lines all the way through the first 45 years of your life, which is halfway up the paper, these events have signified where you are today, who you are today. Now look at the empty space ahead of you between 45 and 90 years of age. It's blank! In other words, it's a clean slate! Design it however you want it. Make better choices and be in charge of designing your own future.

♥○♥

Chapter 5

Far From Home

♥○♥

"To be yourself in a world that is constantly trying to make you something else is the greatest accomplishment."

Ralph Waldo Emerson

An Experience To Die For

The day came, a Saturday morning, when my mother left for work at seven in the morning. I sat at the kitchen table, looking at three bottles of sleeping tablets. I was fifteen years old. I had heard that mixing sleeping tablets with alcohol was dangerous, so I knew that mixing these sleeping tablets with wine would have an extra effect on speeding up the dying process.

I ran through my mind one more time, asking myself important questions:

"Am I really done here?"

"Would anyone hurt as a result of me being gone?"

"Did I miss anything?"

"What will my mother say?"

I was in such a dark place that by this time I didn't care about the impact my being gone would have on my sister. I felt so numb and 'dead' inside that none of the questions stirred any answers except the last one. I knew that my mother would be upset if she found the dirty glass in the sink. *'I better clean it out and put it away. And I better go through the house one more time to make sure everything is clean,'* I thought to myself.

Even in this down-and-out abyss I wanted to prevent my mother from getting angry at me. I had never figured out why she seemed always so absent minded and angry. All my life I felt that I was the cause of her anger and unhappiness. The pressure had become too much. It was time to go home.

I poured 87 prescription strength sleeping tablets into a 10 ounce glass and crunched them up with the back of a knife. I filled the glass with red wine and waited a minute or two while stirring the thick, pink soup of poison. Turning my back and leaning against the kitchen counter I raised the glass and started to drink what must be by far the most disgusting substance I could have ever mixed together. As I was drinking this thick, creamy, sandy textured tincture, I felt a huge bubble of heat outside of me right in front of my belly and stomach area. It felt as if someone was holding a huge candle in front of my stomach. I kept looking down to see what this heat was but didn't see anything.

Drinking the last drop I said: *"It is finished."*

I had no emotions, I was completely numb. I cleaned the glass and the knife and put everything back in its place. Then I went in my room and still in my pajamas I laid down. I wanted to lay in a position where no one would have to find a stiff body but find my body in a way where I could just fit into a casket and be buried or cremated.

As I laid there I now I felt at peace, I was ready to what felt like going home. I was looking forward to ending this useless suffering, this life that simply made no sense to me.

Some random thoughts went through my head but I didn't pay attention. All I wanted was to fall asleep. I felt content.

Suddenly I heard this most familiar voice that had accompanied me throughout my childhood. I had asked it to leave me when I was twelve, but here it was again. It asked in a loud, firm voice:

"What if you just made the biggest mistake of your life?"

I hadn't heard the voice for so long and was angry at the voice for taking my Dad and tearing my family apart, even though there wasn't much of a family, it was all I had known. Up until then it had repeated over and over again that some day something very special was going to happen to me. And when my family fell apart I felt unprepared to go on living. I didn't see the specialness in myself or my life. And I felt that the voice had lied to me. The voice heeded my request and stopped talking to me for all this time.

And yet here it was loud and clear: "*What if you just made the biggest mistake of your life?*"

Along with the voice came flashes of what looked like Polaroid shots of future events. I was given dates and visions of myself at the age of 50 and 86 and everywhere in between. In these visions I looked happy and healthy and content. I owned my life instead of it owning me. In these visions I wanted to live, I had somehow figured out that being here had purpose.

I realized in an instant that my life was to go on, that I hadn't even begun to live. I realized that I was playing the victim, relying on my parents when I was to be the creator of my own life.

But now I had a big problem, I was dying. I had no idea if I had laid down fifteen or thirty minutes ago, all I knew was that I had a huge problem. My body was dying, but my spirit suddenly wanted to live.

In a firm tone the voice said: "*Get up, hurry, you don't have much time.*"

I threw on my clothes and knew I was running for my life, literally. I ran half a mile to the bus stop where two different buses

stopped every hour, one of which would go straight to the hospital. It was a Saturday and the bus schedule was much more scarce on Saturdays, I had no idea if I would have to wait for the bus and if I would make it. What I did know is that my body started to get very heavy and very sleepy. I could barely run, my body felt like a brick weighing a ton.

In absolute divine timing just as I got to the bus stop the right bus, which would take me straight to the hospital, pulled up. Truly the entire sequence of events was orchestrated by heavenly angels. Today looking back I realize how blessed I really was and continue to be.

While I was sitting on the bus, which seemed to take forever to get to the hospital, my mind was trying to go a million miles an hour.

"Will I make it? What if I don't make it?"

This was way before the age of cell phones. There was no one to call, no one to inform. My body was aching, heavy and I was fighting to keep my eyes open. I felt like closing my eyes and just letting go, I was still torn about wanting to live because I wanted to go back to that beautiful golden light I remembered from when I died ten years earlier. The powerful rings and waves of the voice were unmistakable and I knew I needed to follow the visions and instructions.

Finally the bus stopped and I had a little further to walk before I reached the hospital. I remember trying to run but the heaviness and sleepiness of my body felt so surreal that frankly I don't even know how I made it into the hospital lobby. The sliding glass doors opened and I grabbed the first nurse that walked across the hospital lobby telling her what I did. Then I collapsed. I don't

remember even hitting the floor but I do remember my last thought:

"I want to die."

♥0♥0♥0♥0♥0♥0♥0♥0♥0♥0♥0♥0♥0♥0♥0♥0♥0♥0♥0♥0♥0♥0♥0♥0♥0♥0♥0♥0♥0♥0♥0♥0♥0♥0♥

Chapter 6

Dead End Street

♥○♥

"You are searching the world for treasures but the real treasure is yourself."

Rumi

Urgent Information About Suicide

In my teenage ignorance I wanted to find a way back to heaven by means of suicide and expected an overdose of sleeping tablets to just help me drift off. Death by sleeping pills is never peaceful. No path of suicide is peaceful. The following information may give you some more insights on how our bodies actually die through various suicide methods:

Death by Overdose:

An overdose of sleeping tablets do make you drowsy and you will fall asleep at first. However, you will wake up again because your body's natural defense mechanism is to rid itself of the poison. It will attempt to make you vomit out the poison. However, the overdose of chemical substances in your body will have paralyzed your body's muscles and so prevent you from actually vomiting, hence, death occurs through drowning of your own vomit.

Death by Aspirin:

An overdose of aspirin will make you drown in your own blood. Aspirin's main ingredient is a blood thinning substance. And overdose of this substance will cause your blood to become so thin that it will permeate through your veins into every part of your body, including your lungs. Your lungs will fill up with blood and death occurs through drowning in your own blood.

Death by Tylenol:

The same as above. In addition, as few as 15 Tylenol sleeping tablets cause permanent liver damage.

Jumping off the Golden Gate Bridge:

Many think that jumping off the Golden Gate Bridge will cause immediate death. Some people even believe that the fall itself will cause the person to lose consciousness before they ever hit the water. While falling off such heights will feel like you've hit a concrete floor, every bone in your body will instantly break the moment of impact but you most likely will be alive at impact. Because your bones are broken, however, you are not able to swim to safety and cause of death is most likely by drowning.

Pulling the Trigger:

Unfortunately more and more people resort to more definite and drastic measures of committing suicide. Using a gun often fails as death is not always assured. In many cases life continues but serious brain damage occurs. Now not only do you continue living but you now are a vegetable, perhaps even brain dead.

THERE IS NO WAY TO PEACEFULLY COMMIT SUICIDE!

As someone once said: *"The problems you are now facing are temporary, suicide is permanent."*

Suicide is never, ever the answer! Please use your head, reach out and talk to someone. If the first person doesn't seem to get it, continue asking for help until you get the help you need.

If you are in the United States call 1-800-SUICIDE. They are here to help you 24 hours a day, 7 days a week.

A Few Facts About Suicide

92% of people committing suicide prove to have either been diagnosed with a mental health condition and/or are on medication. A person with suicide in their family is 50% more likely to attempt suicide as well. The person with the highest suicide success rate is a white male in his 60s or older. Men are 3-4 times as likely to commit suicide with more definite measures, such as using a gun, hanging, jumping off bridges. Women use less drastic measures but attempt suicide more frequently. Suicide is on the rise in alarming rates amongst people of all ages.

Please familiarize yourself with these facts and never undermine someone reaching out to you for help. If you don't know how to help, call 1-800-SUICIDE (within the United States) and ask how to help your friend or family member.

Common Misconceptions about Suicide

FALSE: People who talk about suicide won't really do it. Almost everyone who commits or attempts suicide has given some clue or warning. Do not ignore suicide threats. Statements like *"you'll be sorry when I'm dead,"* *"I can't see any way out,"* - no matter how casually or jokingly said may indicate serious suicidal feelings.

FALSE: Anyone who tries to kill him/herself must be crazy. Most suicidal people are not psychotic or insane. They must be upset, grief-stricken, depressed or despairing, but extreme distress and emotional pain are not necessarily signs of mental illness.

FALSE: If a person is determined to kill him/herself, nothing is going to stop them.

Even the most severely depressed person has mixed feelings about death, wavering until the very last moment between wanting to live and wanting to die. Most suicidal people do not want death; they want the pain to stop. The impulse to end it all, however overpowering, does not last forever.

FALSE: People who commit suicide are people who were unwilling to seek help.

Studies of suicide victims have shown that more than half had sought medical help in the six months prior to their deaths.

FALSE: Talking about suicide may give someone the idea. You don't give a suicidal person morbid ideas by talking about suicide. The opposite is true - bringing up the subject of suicide and discussing it openly is one of the most helpful things you can do.

Source: SAVE - Suicide Awareness Voices of Education

♥O♥O♥O♥O♥O♥O♥O♥O♥O♥O♥O♥O♥O♥O♥O♥O♥O♥O♥O♥O♥O♥O♥O♥O♥O♥O♥O♥O♥O♥

Chapter 7

The Love of Source

♥○♥

"A teacher is never a giver of truth; he is a guide, a pointer to the truth that each student must find for himself."

Bruce Lee

Second Near Death Experience

It was 1981. I was 15 years old. The hospital's automatic sliding doors opened and I ran across the clean floor towards the first nurse I saw on the other side of the lobby. I knew I was dying and that I may have only minutes left to live.

As I approached the nurse I remember thinking to myself: "Was this all life had to offer?" And I remember feeling disappointed.

As soon as I reached the nurse I felt the world drift away as if in slow motion, just in time to grab her white coat. Everything in my periphery started to twirl and become liquid, as if someone took a brush and distorted the image. I remember thinking:

"I want to die."

I remembered collapsing but I was out before hitting the floor.

Suddenly I found myself floating in a tunnel.

'I remember this place,' I remember thinking to myself. *'I've been here before.'* It was a strange and yet a comforting feeling of déjà vu. Although I don't remember floating through a tunnel the first time around when I was five years old, the feeling and level of consciousness was just the same in this place. I vividly remembered coming back to this life and asking my mother if I was dead. I remember disagreeing with her when she said: "Of course you're not dead." I remember questioning her about this and 'that other life' and tried to convince her that this was just a dream and that the 'other life' was real.

Here I found myself again, ten years later, floating in this all too familiar tunnel and I felt extreme happiness to finally be here in this blissful space once again. I vaguely remembered the voice that just a few hours earlier asked me if I had just made the biggest mistake of my life. No, this was not a mistake. This was exactly where I wanted to be, this felt like home. I quickly decided that it was time to let go of the visions this voice had brought me. It didn't matter that I saw a happy, beautiful woman at the age of 50 and an even happier woman at the age of 86. I was 15 and my physical life had just ended and I was getting ready to go back to heaven where I belonged.

The feeling of being in this tunnel and seeing this ineffable light at the end of it is literally indescribable. The light is so powerful and so strong that it seemed a billion times brighter than the sun and yet I was able to look at it without discomfort. In fact, my entire body felt light and airy, as if non existent. I looked at my right hand and realized that the density of my 'body' was nothing like it is in this physical realm, I seemed to be merely a mist, almost translucent. I looked down on my feet and didn't see any feet, there seemed to be an energetic gown of some sort covering my feet. I also realized that there was no bottom to this tunnel, my feet weren't touching anything. I was floating. I was fascinated and in awe.

I looked at the light at the end of the tunnel and knew I needed to become one with this amazing energy. I wanted to get there faster but no matter how hard I tried to speed up floating through this tunnel, it was as if I was carried along this tunnel in slow motion.

Overcome by the feeling that I had been here before, I started to look around and ask questions. I was fascinated by the tunnel because although it looked like a tunnel I didn't see any bricks. I

remember trying to look at the wall intensely and asking myself: 'What is this?' Suddenly I was 'in' the wall looking at myself floating through the tunnel! I was surprised to see myself from the 'outside', my consciousness was the tunnel and I yet my consciousness was also the misty illusion of this translucent body floating through this gateway.

The next thing I realized was that there is no wall. I was the wall. I was inside the tunnel but there was no separation between the wall and the space in between the translucent being that I saw in front of me.

I looked at my own persona floating through the tunnel as if I was the tunnel wall looking at myself. I remember asking myself: 'Which am I, the wall or this body?' Suddenly I was back in my body looking at the wall again. Although I seemed to be slipping from one point in the tunnel to another, the feeling of being everywhere at the same time stayed the same. As I was in the wall looking at myself, the memory of who I was retained in that consciousness of me now being in the wall.

I remember being fascinated with this and completely not understanding of what was happening. I remember asking: 'How is this possible? What is this place?'

Suddenly I felt as if there was a split happening and I was in the wall and in my body at the same time, looking both at my body and at the wall from my body at the same time. It was like being in multiple places at the same time, without any effort at all.

I remember looking at the space between 'me' and the tunnel and asking: 'Then what is this space?' And suddenly I was neither my body nor the tunnel and my consciousness or awareness was in the in-between space while at the same time being in my body

and the wall. I was absolutely amazed, fascinated and overcome with joy. I seemed to shift consciousness into whatever place I wanted to be and yet my memory stayed with me and yet it also stayed with the body and the tunnel.

I looked at the light and I remembered suddenly that everything in this place was an illusion. My body floating through that tunnel, the wall, the in-between space, my physical life that I just left behind, it was all an illusion. I didn't realize it until I looked into that bright, golden-white light and I just knew that the only reality would be found when I would reach this light.

I was overcome with love looking at the light and I didn't care what was behind me, I only cared to be one with this light. I wanted to be immersed in it, become one with it, melt into it, dissolve into it, I didn't want to exist anymore, I just wanted to be one with that love that I felt coming from this light.

Suddenly I was overtaken by the most amazing humming of what sounded like hundreds of thousands of angels' voices. I wasn't aware of these voices when I first found myself in this tunnel. I remember feeling utterly overcome by the deepest sense of unconditional love that I had ever experienced. I felt like breaking down onto my knees in utter humility, I felt like crying but not because it hurt to hear these voices, but because I felt like I was melting and dissolving into nothingness. I remember looking around to see the angels but I couldn't see anything. Suddenly my conscious was leaving my body and while drifting upwards my consciousness was turning into the voices themselves. To date this is the hardest piece to explain because there just are not enough words (or the right words) to explain what it feels like to become a music note. It felt like the ultimate melting experience and it was as if I was riding the waves of sound.

I noticed as my consciousness became the humming tunes and I became each individual wave and musical pitch, while looking at my body, that my body became like an energetic wave of sorts. The transparency now was clearly visible, I looked like an illusion. I realized that the orbs of the voices and I were one and the voices themselves and I were one. They were sound waves, like round spheres. Except these sound spheres were everywhere and seemingly coming out of nowhere and yet they permeated this entire place. They touched everything and yet they didn't exist and somehow they made everything visible. It was like a gazillion tiny rainbow atoms together singing the most beautiful symphony and I was its creator, its conductor and its final creation.

At an instant I realized it was the vibration of these voices that were carrying me through the tunnel and that in fact the entire illusion of the tunnel, the vision of my own body, the space in between me and the walls of the tunnel, everything, was created because of these voices. They were the same rings of sound that I had been feeling or seeing since I was little, only here there were so many of them that they seemed to create the entire reality of this place.

I heard the all too familiar voice: *"Find the key to instant manifestations."*

Not knowing what was meant I did know the key was to be found within sound. One thing was clear:

All matter is created with sound.

Still floating through the tunnel while riding sound waves, I was shown snippets of certain things, visions you could call them, barely split seconds long, but long enough for me to realize that

with sound this universe was created and it is with sound that this universe is being destroyed. I realized that every word and thought and movement that emanates from my heart, my mind and my mouth is a force of life or a force of destruction, no exception.

What key was he talking about?

It would take me three decades to find the key.

Back in my 'floating body' I was now determined more than ever to become one with this blissful light ahead of me. I continued floating through the tunnel looking at this most amazing bright light in front of me, which only seemed to become more magnificent the closer I got. All I wanted was to jump into this light and become one with it as fast as I could.

I didn't think about what to expect when I got to the light. I don't remember thinking about heaven or hell or wondering if there would be judgment. I didn't wonder what it would be like, whom I would see or if anyone was waiting for me. All I wanted was to lose myself, to surrender to life and death itself, to be the light itself.

Approaching the light I stretched out my right hand in preparation to become one with the light. When I finally reached the end of the tunnel my right middle finger touched the light first and immediately it was as if I plugged into a massive computer system or some kind of system where all reality and knowledge exists. I watched my right hand as my fingers one by one became immersed in the light and at the same time my hand melted away into the light.

Out of the light came a massive, transparent looking like cube that first enveloped my right arm and then my entire being. Major information was downloaded into my 'system' as if by means of 'blocks of information.' I saw visions flash before or inside of my awareness, visions of the future, visions of how the world is created, visions of our magnificence. I was truly overwhelmed with the visions this cube contained and what I saw, I didn't know if I wanted to see any of it or what I was supposed to do with it all. All I wanted was to dissolve into this light.

Just when I felt as I was able to immerse into this light, a violent pull from behind and against my will was pulling me back through the tunnel and away from the light. The tunnel and the voices and everything in it were pulled away from me right in front of my eyes and became smaller and smaller and smaller. Everything happened so fast and I remember calling out saying: "No!!!"

Back In the Body

Meanwhile, my physical body had been laying in a hospital bed for four days and although the resuscitation was successful, I had missed four days of human life. My hearing came back first, my body was a bit slower to wake up but my consciousness was alert and fully awake. I opened my eyes. And I was angry, disappointed and sad because I was well aware that I was nowhere in some heavenly abode but somewhere back in this physical body. Life would continue but I had no answers or ideas as to which direction I was supposed to go in.

I spent the next three years in serious depression and reminiscing about my experiences in the tunnel. It was difficult wanting to live in this physical body after this experience and frankly I didn't

really know what to do on this planet after this experience. My inner life to this point had been kept a secret and my outer life was not reflective or inclusive of my sacred time in the tunnel. There was no one to speak to about these two worlds. The seen world, which seemed real but I knew it was such an illusion, and the unseen world, which seemed like such an illusion to humans but seemed so real to me.

The tunnel is alive and well. Today I call it the worm hole or time warp for adults to transition from one realm to another. Today I see worm holes of various kinds to travel between worlds, from the future back to what we call 'now' and worm holes that lead through the gate within the sun.

The touching of the light was essential and is alive also as it makes 'tuning into' Source more crisp and clear. Like a radio station that comes through fully and clearly and without static. When I want information all that is needed is to ride the waves of sound or go 'back' to the blocks of information that are constantly being downloaded.

Over the decades since this experience I have had only two missions:

1. To find the key of instant manifestation as I was instructed and

2. To be the unconditional love that I was blessed enough to experience when riding those sound waves so that I can help souls in their evolutionary journey

The Love of Source

Many believe that unless one is a mother one does not know true love, and nothing can be further from that truth. As a mother myself even the love of a mother cannot possibly come close to the type of love that Source is, that we are, that is all around us and in us at all times. True, unconditional love is not reserved only for mothers. Men, animals, insects, plants, likewise, have the capability of knowing this endless source of unconditional love. It is not a type of love that springs from giving birth with our body, in fact, it is a type of love that 'just is' and its source is within. It does not need to be worked for, nor does it restrict itself to 'good' people or 'deserving' people. Just like the sun shines on the entire planet and all human beings, the murderer and the *innocent* little infants, unconditional love shines from within all of us, without playing favoritism or placing judgment on people. We are the ones who block the fountain of love that is within us and wants to overflow with this river of love. When we learn that **"love does not come to us from the horizon but love spreads from within us far beyond the horizon,"** as Lao Russell so beautifully stated, we will learn that we are the Source of love.

Unfortunately the type of love that humans associate with has hatred as its counter part. Human love is usually conditional and based on greed. That's why couples who used to love each other at one point can suddenly turn and hate each other.

It is from this fountain I attempt and re-attempt to live my daily life from while occupying this physical temple. It is with this type of unconditional love that I get up and do my work.
I do have a vision and dream for all humanity:

"For every soul on this planet to walk free to evolve, expand and experience their true magnificence."

Back Home

I was in the hospital for over a week. When it was time to be released I took the same bus home. The door was locked, I ran the door bell. My mother opened the door just enough so I could see her one stern eye peak through the door. With the coldness of ice in her eyes she said:

"Do you know how stupid you made me look in front of the neighbors!? It's obvious you need more responsibilities. You either start paying rent or it's time for you to move out."

After my Dad left when I was twelve I was asked to get my first paid job. I would no longer be getting any food beyond the basic items, and I would have to pay for my own clothes. One day a week and every school vacation I drove my bicycle for 45 minutes one way to go to work in a small convenience store stocking shelves. Ever since I was twelve I worked every summer until I had enough money to buy a moped as soon as I turned fourteen. I felt blessed not to have to ride my bicycle so far to work.

I felt empowered to earn my own money, no matter how little it was. The little I earned was hardly enough to buy my own food and clothes and gas for my moped, but now I needed to pay rent? How could I possibly do that?

I had some thinking to do.

A Knock on the Door

My mother left every Saturday at 7 a.m. to go to work and she didn't return until later in the afternoon. About an hour after she left there was a knock on the door. The door was locked and I thought perhaps my mother had forgotten something. I opened the door and pushing through the door was a grown man who proceeded to chase me down the hall and into the living room. I was only fifteen and he was a grown man in his twenties, I was still in my pajamas and there was no way I could outrun him, there was no way to go.

He tackled me to the ground in the living room and sat on top of my fighting body while squeezing my wrists into the rough, copper colored carpet. As I looked into his dark eyes I suddenly saw flashes of photographs of women, men and children who had fallen victim at the hands of violators. Domestic violence, child abuse, prisoners - it was all there in a blink of an eye. And I was terrified and overwhelmed by the agony of what I saw.

I did not have the strength to scream, it took all my strength to move my body around with every ounce of strength I had so he knew that the moment he let go of one of my hands I would fight for my life. I tried kicking up my legs but wasn't able to reach him.

The visions of all these victims were so overwhelming that in an instant I remembered all the disappointment I had felt for this life, the hatred towards my parents for not staying together, not wanting me, for not ever hearing 'I love you.' I felt the energy coil up within me and I was going to give this man the fight of his life. For as long as I was alive there was no way I would let him get away with what he was here to accomplish. I took in a deep breath and as I was about to give him all of my energy at once his eyes got frightened at what he saw in my eyes. I don't know what

he saw but he looked scared for his life, he jumped off and ran down the hallway. And I ran after him! I was so angry at the audacity of him coming into my house and wanting to violate me in the way he had intended, there was no way I was going to let him get away without a beating.

I ran after him down the hallway and out the door when suddenly I realized how careless I was being. I immediately went back inside, locked the door and took inventory of my aching wrists burning with rug burns, red and aching.

This incident was all I needed to let me know that I was no longer safe in this environment. I had to leave and live on own. I made the fateful decision that I might as well leave school and move out on my own. I disliked school and I didn't feel safe being at home, paying rent seemed impossible. I decided to drop out of eight grade and start living my own life.

♥O♥O♥O♥O♥O♥O♥O♥O♥O♥O♥O♥O♥O♥O♥O♥O♥O♥O♥O♥O♥O♥O♥O♥O♥O♥O♥O♥O♥O♥

Chapter 8

I Want To Live

♥○♥

"Your body is woven from the light of heaven."

Rumi

Life Continues and Turns 'Normal'

The three years before the attempted suicide were ridden with a different kind of depression. It was a depression filled with pain and agony of having to live a life that I seemingly never signed up for. The three years after my suicide attempt were ridden with a completely different kind of depression and didn't resemble the same dark energies as the previous three years at all. The loneliness felt different too. Suddenly there were these insights from the 'other side' that I was unable to share with anyone. Instead of contemplating suicide, because I knew that suicide was not the answer, I started to pray to God that he would just end my life the 'right way.' I just wanted to be home and at peace and in a place that felt so much more real to me than this illusionary world. I prayed and prayed and prayed, but I never got an answer.

Moving Out At Fifteen

Instead of continuing useless school and trying to work even more just so I could pay rent I decided to move an hour away and into a horse back riding stable where I had a room above the horses. I worked hard, got up at four and worked until six. Between 6:30 and 7:00 the worker got breakfast before returning to work until eleven. We got lunch at noon and returned back to work from four in the afternoon until ten at night. Afternoons were spent riding horses. I put in 19 hour work days, five days a week. With my body have crumbled as much as it did because of the cortisone I didn't last long and soon started to notice that I couldn't even hold a toothbrush. Everything dropped out of my hands. I was put on disability and both of my arms put in casts after a doctor diagnosed me with severe chronic carpal tunnel.

I never talked about the man coming into my house and bruising my wrists. There was no one to talk to. I was sure had I told my mother she would have scolded me for opening the door in the first place. "Why bother," I remember recalling.

The visions, however, of the victims falling prey to men with less honorable intentions haunted me for decades. I realized that the physical hurt he caused to my wrists in combination with the visions were causing me to lose all strength in my hands.

For three decades I was unable to wear watches, bracelets or be touched around my wrists without going into a panic. It never bothered me until someone touched my wrists when I finally realized how much of a prisoner I still was to this event. I had not dealt with it thoroughly. I had forgiven the man, yes, but I didn't know how to deal with the pain of all the victims I saw, knowing that this abuse is happening every second of the day somewhere around the globe. I needed to take a serious ostrich approach and stick my head in the sand, dealing with this reality was simply too much for me, I just didn't know how to handle it.

Until nearly thirty years later when I finally learned an important lesson, which I will share in more detail later when I talk about the "four doors." When I finally learned that it was not enough to face my fears but that I also needed to master my fears, was when I began to look at this event again, this time in much detail. It didn't take long for me to take the energy of this event and turn it into something beautiful for everyone. I will share more later.

Two months later my casts came off and with a saddened heart was told that I would never do heavy physical labor again. The damage to my soft tissues was beyond repair. With a broken heart I now was homeless and going back to my mother was not

an option. I decided to move away even farther away and take a job as a live-in maid with a French speaking family. At least I would be learning French and it would give me some time to think of what I wanted to do next.

The cleaning and cooking for four was too painful for my hands and it became clear that my time was limited here as well.

I was seventeen now and had been living on my own for two years, floundering, not knowing where life was going. My dream to work with horses had come to an end, physical labor had become too strenuous. A check up at the medical University left me with the diagnosis of deteriorating soft tissue disease, a form of rheumatism. No seventeen year old should have rheumatism, there had to be a way.

I decided to move to Zürich and was accepted into a two year customer service degree program from the government of Switzerland. Learning French had paid off, it was the only pre-requisite to get enrolled in the program. There was hope.

I Want To Live!

I turned eighteen and made the decision that I could either live life depressed and lonely or that I could get my act together and do my best here while in this body. I decided to live, perhaps for the first time in life.

I joined a gym and within a few weeks I had my first boyfriend. We got engaged and moved in together when I was twenty. Our relationship only lasted three years because his idea for us was that I would be a stay-home mom, clean and cook and raise his children. My idea of a fulfilled life was more like *"let's travel the*

world and learn new languages." We parted ways and off I went to realize my dreams.

Forgiveness

Before life could go on I felt the urgent need to forgive my parents. I knew I needed forgiveness too. I had not talked to or heard from my father since I was twelve. I stopped contact with my mother after I moved out at the age of fifteen. I was an adult now and it was time to be my own adult, to take responsibility. It was time to shed this enormously heavy backpack with all these unnecessary rocks in them, this lack of forgiveness. I never knew what I did to my parents for them to be the way they are, but this didn't change the fact that it was me that was harboring just as much resentment, anger and bitterness. And it was this energy that I wanted to get rid of.

I contacted my parents, one at a time, and attempted to reconcile. I asked for forgiveness and even asked to see my Dad. It did not go as planned and as I had hoped, our relationship remained non-existent and estranged. Fathers can't just make their way back into a girls life when they were absent during a girl's most important unfolding time - the time of their teenage years. I tried, he tried, but at this time it seemed just not doable.

My mother was cold as always and it would take me more decades to fully understand her.

I had done my best to forgive and get forgiveness. It was time to live my life and move on and to focus on my own life.

My first stop was the Italian part of Switzerland. I already spoke Swiss German, High German and French by this time. Next, I went

to work for a private Swiss Bank in the Italian part of Switzerland, close to Como, where I learned Italian.

My next stop was the United States. I was 23 years old when I arrived in San Francisco with only two suitcases and $500 in my pocket and speaking no English, I embarked on a brand new life in a completely different culture. I learned English watching Oprah and at night time I returned to the local College to take Spanish classes.

Soon I fell in love and a wedding was planned only a year away. Life was great and I was glad to be alive.

Life's Hurdles

All went well, my English was improving and our small, ten person family wedding started to take shape. I was happy and healthy and happy to be alive!

Three weeks before the wedding, however, I started to get sick and had my first surgery. A few days later I had another emergency surgery. A few days later I had my third emergency surgery, back surgery. It was only six days to our wedding.

Three emergency surgeries in less than three weeks! What was going on?

Clearly, the Universe did not want me to get married, so we cancelled the wedding.

Heeding Spirit's Interference

We often get mad at God for 'taking away' something we wanted so badly. Whether it's that dream job, dream boyfriend or girlfriend, dream house, whatever it is, when we don't get it, we usually react and get mad at God, feeling as though God has a bone to pick with us or doesn't want us to be happy.

Nothing could be further from the Truth. Quite the contrary is true. After memorizing and making a permanent program the following mantra, **'I am divinely guided and protected and always in the right place at the right time,'** I have learned to trust God explicitly and when I don't seem to get something, I thank Source in advance for spearing me a less than ideal outcome. I may never know what the outcome would have been had I forced my way, and I'm in a place where I don't want to know anymore, I simply trust that there is something bigger or better coming my way.

Unfortunately, this lesson I had not yet learned as of this time, and I was determined to live my life by forcing my way. I used to call it having strong 'will power' or 'not giving up.' Today I just see it for what it is: beating my head against the wall when instead all I need to do is wait patiently with open arms to receive that which is seeking me as much as I am seeking it and wants to come to me at high speed.

Try it, you might be surprised to see how fast blessings can materialize and show up before you as if by magic. The Universe does like speed.

♥O♥O♥O♥O♥O♥O♥O♥O♥O♥O♥O♥O♥O♥O♥O♥O♥O♥O♥O♥O♥O♥O♥O♥O♥O♥O♥O♥O♥O♥O♥

Chapter 9

Three Knocks On The Door

♥0♥0♥0♥0♥0♥0♥0♥0♥0♥0♥0♥0♥0♥0♥0♥0♥0♥0♥0♥0♥0♥0♥0♥0♥0♥0♥0♥0♥0♥0♥0♥0♥0♥

"You were born to light up this world. When you were born you gifted this world with something that was not here before."

Anonymous

My Third Near Death Experience

The day after I came home from the hospital I attempted to take my first shower. My fiancé helped me over the ledge of the bathtub by holding my hands while I stepped inside the tub. He sat outside of the bathroom ready to help me out of the shower as soon as I was done.

It felt good to take my first shower when suddenly the world in my periphery started to twirl and get distorted. I had seen this twirling of *reality* one too many times and instantly knew that I was dying.

'I'm dying! Shit, not again!' I remember thinking to myself.

I called my fiancé with an urgent tone in my voice struggling to stay in my body for just another couple of seconds, he immediately entered the bathroom.

"Hold me," were my last words. I don't even remember falling, I suddenly found myself in this beautiful, blissful place with rich, orange colors and clouds everywhere. It felt as if I was floating somewhere above in the clouds but I knew that it wasn't in this reality, and yet it wasn't the same familiar feel than what I experienced during my first and second near death experience. This somehow felt like it belonged to someone else's heaven. I remember asking myself: *"Are we creating our own heavens?"*

There wasn't anyone around, it was just me.

I looked down but couldn't see anything besides clouds. As far as I looked all I saw were orange, puffy clouds that looked like golden orange, misty cotton balls. Suddenly I saw a man sitting at

a far distance. I don't know what he was sitting on, I didn't see a bench, but he was definitely sitting and resting his elbows on his knees. He was wearing a white robe and with a telepathic message summoned me to come closer.

As I approached him I noticed that I was floating. It was as if by my mere thought and willingness to approach him I was moving my presence towards him, even though I wasn't moving my legs or arms. I looked at my hands and they didn't seem as translucent as in my second near death experience, I seemed more solid. I also didn't wear a robe.

As I stood close to him he gave me a telepathic message to be passed on to a living person. I promised to deliver the message when from behind me at a far, far away distance I heard my fiancé's voice call for me. He kept calling for me: **"Please come back to me."**

Turning to see where the voice came from I couldn't see my fiancé, I only kept hearing his desperate plea to return. Turning my head towards the man I said: *"I promise to pass on the message but I have to go now."*

"Yes, you do," he said.

In a similar way the way I woke up after my second near death experience I felt my consciousness back in my body but was unable to move or even feel my body. I just knew I was back and I kept hearing my fiancé's desperate attempts to get me to do or say something. I wasn't able to speak or even open my eyes but he saw my lips move and he yelled: *"She's back!"*

By the time I opened my eyes the fire department was making their way into the room as they surrounded my fiancé holding my

naked body in his arms. It was time for him to let me go and let the paramedics do their work.

What made this so difficult for my fiancé was that his father had died in his arms the same way. His head fell back, he took his last breath and his eyes rolled back in his eyes. When I said *"hold me"* he thought I wanted a hug, but as my body collapsed and my body fell backwards with my eyes and mouth opened, he knew that I had died because he had seen this look before. He was beside himself.

On my way back to the hospital I vomited all over the ambulance. The emergency room doctors confirmed that I had overdosed on too much anesthesia.

Rather than keeping our wedding postponed I decided that not even death was going to prevent me from marrying the man I had promised to marry. We called city hall and got married in the living room of my fiancé's mother with just his mom and sister as witnesses. After the vows were exchanged I went back to bed. We never had a 'white wedding' and never had a honey moon. Life together became so much more important than spending money we didn't have on stuff we didn't need. There would be money and time to have a honey moon later.

Grateful for yet another chance at life my spiritual channels opened even more. I was hungry to talk to someone about it and did my best to try to talk to my husband about it. Unfortunately my 'other, unseen worlds' were not welcomed and embraced as much as I had hoped and this world remained one I would not be able to share with my marriage partner.

Being In Touch With Your Mortality

There are way too many people who are inundating themselves with information but pay not a fraction as much of attention to their own personal transformation. And yet transformation is what we are all here for. To be in touch with our mortality on a constant basis is key to living a rich, full life. Life is so incredibly fragile, we don't even have the slightest idea as to when our physical life is suddenly over. We live our lives as if we are going on living forever, and we do, at least our soul does, but the challenge is that most of us are not in touch with the part of us that goes on living forever: the soul. And instead we live like our bodies go on living forever when clearly our body is just an organic mechanism that is here today and gone tomorrow. Our four layered body temples are just organic matter that is built from the same stuff mother Nature grows her plants and flowers. Our bodies are no different. And the refolding and recycling of these vessels is inevitable. The questions is not 'if' you're going to die but 'when and how' are you going to die. And only you can answer this question because deep within you already know the answer to this question.

Stop Chasing The Skirts, Drugs and Other Nonsense

The majority of humanity defines their beingness, their very existence, as if they have eternity to live in their physical bodies. Proof of this is the constant chasing after sense oriented behaviors. Food, sex, pleasures of the flesh, the materialism, the need to impress our neighbors or worse, strangers, with stuff we don't even need.

Fake has been 'in' for a long time and it seems as though the whole planet has caught on to this character fashion statement. There are not enough people left who are keeping it real. It's time now to see the fakeness in these illusions and to get down to what is real. Your soul, my soul, her soul, his soul - everyone's soul.

Voltaire says: **"It is difficult to free fools from the chains they revere."**

It is time now to let go of the false security, bliss and happiness that materialism promises us to bring. Rumi says that **"you are searching the world for treasures but the real treasure is yourself."**

Why are you so afraid of silence?

Why are you so afraid to see the brilliant light that you really are?

The Light That You Are

If you are still stuck on reading magazines that only serve to make you feel uglier than you already feel, it's time to remember that you are beautiful from within, not because of the shape of your vessel, but because of the ineffable volume of soul that your body temple houses. When you were born, you brought a gift to this planet that was not here before you came - a light so bright that it can never be extinguished. It is now time to know your true beauty, to meet your true self, and to gift the world with this most sacred light of yours. There is no competition to what you are here to do, because only you know how to play your instrument. Play it - it's time and the time is NOW.

It is time now to direct our attention to the treasures within, which is where the real action is taking place. The majority of humanity needs a serious wake up call in form of a disease within ourselves or a deadly illness in someone we love, before we wake up. Most of us need to turn elderly before we get what life is all about, and even then we find people who have had a life time of chance after chance to gain wisdom but have gained nothing but bitterness, disappointments and a terrifying fear of death because we finally come to realize that our soul never had a chance to really express itself.

It is time to change this now, loved ones. The time to change this is now, not when you're sick, not when someone you love is dying, not when the world is experiencing another massive earthquake or tsunami or deadly virus or a missile attack or solar flare that will claim millions or billions of lives.

Allow Your Soul To Speak and Expand

Preparing for the worst is going to save neither your soul nor your physical body when the world experiences a massive population reduction, whether the planet is hit by meteorites, a sun flare or man made destruction.

So your life then is important because your body is indeed your vehicle for awakening, however, what is more important is your soul and its evolution.

What is your soul here to experience? Do you even know? Have you ever tuned into your soul to listen to what it wants?

Do you pray for others to have a happy and healthy life or do you pray for the salvation of their souls?

I will speak more of soul harvesting in another chapter. If you have read this far I congratulate you for being curious enough to see where this is going. Where I envision you being right now is within you looking for the answers I just asked you. Retreat to that holy and sacred place within you, it is where all the treasures of the world are contained. All your answers are there. All your answers are also always contained within your questions.

Ask and you shall received. And remember that when you ask you must ask with **all** of your heart, with **all** of your mind and **all** of your body. The answer is always right there for your grasping. Start asking questions!

♥○♥

Chapter 10

And The Two Shall Become One

♥○♥

"I would like my life to be a statement of love and compassion - where it isn't, that's where my work lies."

Ram Dass

Major Decisions

Life after my third near death experience was easier, much easier. I would lie if I said that I didn't prefer to be on the 'other side' and at the same time my sincere interest in all things metaphysical had enabled me to experience the other side simultaneously to this material world.

When I was twelve and decided not to experience the effects of smoking, drugs, alcohol and one-night stands, I turned in the direction of learning everything there was to learn about the world of metaphysics and energy. I became my biggest topic of study. I was interested in how I operated, and consequently how others operated. I embarked on energetic tools such as dowsing, meditating, dream analysis, the I-Ching, color therapy, hypnotherapy, mind focus and concentration and many other modalities, whatever would help me integrate the unseen world with the seen world. There had to be a way to bridge the two worlds. I somehow knew that finding balance between the two would be what could liberate me from feeling so trapped in this physical body. Finding freedom at my inner most core became my sole purpose for existing, which later became my biggest ambition to help others find their own freedom within their own lives.

Marriage and Family

My husband and I were married when I was 25 and I gave birth to a beautiful, gifted girl when I was 27. We soon discovered that she was gifted in unusual ways. Meanwhile my spiritual horizons had expanded to a point where I could hold regular conversations with Beings from the 'other side.' I was given visions that were

clearly not of this world. I wasn't able to communicate them to anyone, but I was at peace asking my inner guides for assistance. When our daughter was born, however, we soon found out that she could see dead people with her regular eyes, to the extreme discomfort of my husband. He wanted no part in what he called 'voodoo crap.'

I was faced with my own memory of being five years old and trying to talk to my mother about what I saw on the 'other side' and being shut down, never having anyone to talk to about what I saw, what I knew, what I was told. Not being able to share all of my life with anyone was the cause of much loneliness in my life. Here I had another opportunity to make a major decision that would shift another human being's life in either *this* direction or *that* direction. What was the right way?

If I decided to obey my husband I would potentially close off an important ability that wanted to have its expression through our daughter. If I decided against his will and nourish my daughter's ability I would certainly cause a rift between myself and my husband, which undoubtedly I would eventually have to explain to my daughter. I felt that no matter what decision I made, there would be a rift in our family unit.

It didn't take much thinking on my part and I knew that the chain that held myself hostage and clearly held my mother hostage too, needed to be broken once and for all. Who knows how many generations came before me who were told that they were crazy or that they were seeing things and were asked to stop 'talking such nonsense.' It was time to stop this judgment and to just let her unfold in her own greatness.

Impacting Time and Space

The moment I made this choice before me appeared thousands and thousands of ancestors who were lining up to extend their gratitude and show their evolution and healing as a result of my decision. It was the first time I realized that the choices I make in this life were impacting not only me and my daughter and those who would come in contact with me throughout my life, they were impacting the past and the power of my decisions were permeating time and space and capable of healing patterns that had been going on for centuries, perhaps thousands of years.

If you find yourself stuck in a pattern that you now are repeating, consider the powerful impact you have by breaking the link in the chain once and for all. This is where true healing on a soul level can take place. Don't be afraid to step up in a big way. Your ancestors will thank you for it and most importantly, your soul gets to live and express its true desires, which is to evolve and expand.

My husband asked not to talk "voodoo crap" in front of him and I agreed that we would not 'practice' our intuitive exercises in front of Dad and so respect his discomfort with the unseen realities that seemed so normal to us.

I literally got another chance to grow up with my daughter in the realm of spirituality. Suddenly there was another human being that saw things similar to me and saw so much more than what I saw. I let her have her own experiences. I asked her questions and to describe what she saw, and I never judged her. Only once did I disbelieve her, and what regrets I have over my attempt to dismiss her ability!

Let me share with you this amazing story.

Chapter 11

Be Careful What You Ask For

♥○♥

"If you want to awaken all of humanity, then awaken all of yourself; if you want to eliminate the suffering of the world then eliminate all that is dark and negative in yourself. Truly the greatest gift you have to give is that of your own self transformation."

Lao Tzu

Reading People's Thoughts

She was seven and I had been practicing to read people's thoughts by doing this simple exercise.

1. Look into a person's third eye and ask your question (mentally).

2. Wait for the answer.

I was so frustrated because no matter how hard I tried I just couldn't get anything. So I called my daughter and gave her the simple task of looking inside my forehead and to ask a silent question. She got an answer almost instantaneously. I completely dismissed it as coincidence. Being the confident little girl she was she wanted to prove it to me. We went out in the backyard where my husband was having a conversation with our neighbor who was leaning over the fence. Our neighbor was doing the talking when my daughter was looking inside his forehead and asked him a silent question. What was remarkable is that she chose the person who was talking rather than the person who was listening. How did she even know that people can do two things at the same time? It never occurred to her that she would never get an answer. This was a major lesson for me.

Within less than 15 seconds she got her answer. Unfortunately there was no way to prove that she was right and I dismissed her from the exercise. Not even a minute after she left to go back inside disappointed that mom did not believe her, our neighbor continued his conversation with my husband when he told him verbatim what my daughter had heard from his subconscious just a minute ago.

With my jaw dropped I literally ran inside to apologize to my daughter, asking her if she could please teach me. Not only did she get an answer to a question, but she got it ahead of time. Where was this answer stored and how did she manage to read something that was obviously only in his subconscious at the time she asked the question?

I was fascinated! We started to call it the mind game. It took me literally an entire month to just hear a simple 'yes' or 'no,' let alone entire sentences. She on the other hand saw the answers typed out across the forehead as if a typewriter was typing out the answers. Even though she was only seven and barely knew how to read, Spirit figured out how to communicate so that she would understand. Unlike most adults children are not judgmental and they are not attached to their answers or how they're being delivered, which is why they are getting answers so much faster.

Be Careful What You Ask For

Out of all the skills I have developed both my daughter and I wish we had never learned this skill. It is the hardest to carry, the most difficult to dismiss and the most horrendous burden to make sense of. For this one simple reason: People's self loathing thoughts are almost unbearable and are so devastating that we both struggled to want to be around people. Our sensitivity towards the outside world became so fine tuned that it became almost painful to be in the presence of people.

While you may think that this is a great ability to have, it is not. Think twice before wanting to get inside someone's head. It's for the most part just negative self talk combined with really

unhealthy and downright destructive thoughts not only about themselves but also about others.

My daughter approached me at the age of eleven, asking if she could just shed all of her 'abilities.' She felt devastated and overwhelmed at hearing the thoughts of her classmates, she felt nauseated knowing some of the things she knew about people while knowing that there was nothing she could do about it. It was decision time once again.

No matter how gifted you or your children are, there may come a time when knowing or seeing certain things are just too much to bear. Acknowledge the burden and respect the decision of someone else wanting to be 'done' with their spiritual journey. It won't last long. It may last a year, two years, five years or a decade. Once a mind has been stretched it can never return to its original state of being.

My daughter and I didn't talk about spiritual things for almost four years when she was ready to admit that even though she had not been talking about it, her spiritual realms had expanded by leaps and bounds. As were mine. We had moved into a place, half of which was literally a highway portal to other realms. All sorts of Beings and spirits were coming through half of our home and we both saw them but out of respect didn't want to talk about them. However, the time came when the spirits were so unique that we just had to talk about them. I was wondering if I was really seeing what I was seeing, talking to someone else who sees as you do is great confirmation. There were new 'things' and Beings she saw too and she needed to talk about them. There was no one in her life whom she could share her experiences with. What was beautiful was that I had seen the same 'things' and it was confirmation for me too that we were indeed growing on our spiritual journeys.

Learning How To Read the Universe's 'Thoughts'

People who read this may go on a mission, thinking that it's pretty 'cool' to read someone else's thoughts. No it's not. It's not only an invasion of privacy, but it's quite damaging and completely without integrity. Instead of reading other people's thoughts, a much more fruitful exercise is to tune into your own soul's hearts. What does your higher self think? Tune into the Universe's heart beat, into our Mother Earth's pulse, into other realms, and see what messages lie there for us. That's where the real information lies. And learning to read the Universe's messages is actually much easier and simpler than turning into another human being's thought patterns.

Today I am quite guarded about picking up human thoughts and other people's thoughts vibrate at a completely different rate and in a different color than the thoughts I create with my own intent. When you start 'seeing' the intricate fabric of the Universe you can easily distinguish between your thoughts, other people's thoughts, thoughts from deceased people or thoughts from aliens, the dark forces and even thoughts from those living in a future time.

Time and space do not exist. They never have, they never will. The only reality is God's static, cold, immovable, white light. The moment there is movement it is a creation of Source. So all that moves, whether in this reality or another, is a creation of Source. What's so difficult for people to understand and accept is that they are Source and at the same time a creation of that very Source. Therefore, you and I create our own reality and we are sharing illusionary space with others who are having their own movement within Source, whether seen with our outer eyes or our inner eyes.

Beings like devils, aliens, ghosts, angels, guides, fairies, gnomes and whatever else you can think up, are automatically real. If you can think of it or imagine it, it is a reality. Period. It's that simple.

We'll talk a little more about this in a later chapter.

Learning To 'See'

Today our daughter is an adult and if we have learned one thing for sure, the language of energy can be learned very easily and very quickly, especially when you have someone you can share your experiences with. The reason it takes so long for adults is because we've been discouraged to believe in the unseen when we were little and especially as adults, and because we distrust our own visions and knowing center as a result of not having that part of us nourished. Self confidence is located in the third chakra, as is self esteem. Both of which are directly tied to our ability to see the unseen. When we don't believe that what we just saw was 'real' and we dismiss it as just a fluke in our imagination, then Spirit will keep us in spiritual pre-school and will not permit us to spiritually advance until we start to believe our own visions. Once we do, we graduate very quickly and start to see, hear and know more.

The language of energy can be learned much quicker with another person whom we can share our visions with. We learn through listening and following other people's visions with our inner eye.

Here is a classic example.

Ghost Dividing Itself

One night I was abruptly woken up by an entity standing by my door. When I looked over I felt a group standing there but only saw one. I was irritated that he was in my bedroom and that he woke me up. My bedroom is sacred and no one but my angelic body guards are permitted in my bedroom when my body is sleeping. I asked him to leave, which he did.

The day after the conversation with my daughter went as follows:

"I had the weirdest ghost in my bedroom last night."

"I saw the weirdest ghost too," she said.

"Really? Tell me about it," I asked.

"I came out of the kitchen and was on my way back to my room when in front of my door I saw this ghost looking straight at me. I told him to move out of the way or I would walk straight through him. I approached but he didn't move. My heart started to beat faster but I was determined to move straight through him if he didn't move. Right as I was getting ready to step into him he literally split into three. I saw him in front of me, to the left of me, to the right of me and then felt him behind me. It was so weird."

I told her that this was exactly what I felt in my room. I looked at him and felt a group standing there but I only saw one.

This ghost became an important teacher to me.

Everyone Is a Teacher

I was fascinated by his ability to split himself into multiple parts of himself. Not only did he teach me something really important about how the dark side works, he also taught me that if they can do it, so can we. As a Reiki master I give long distance Reiki to friends and family and I often appear in their homes rather than bringing them into my space. Suddenly I knew that I was no longer bound by just giving one person long distance healing but I too could split myself into endless versions of myself. What a revelation.

You may have heard of ancient sages who appear to people in various parts of the world. What used to puzzle me before this experience is how they could appear in two or three places at the same time. Now we know.

This was a huge lesson for me as I learned that the street is always endless. It's never a dead-end, a one-way street or even a two-way street, the possibilities are literally endless. It was when I made this realization that I asked Spirit to show me everything my body, mind and heart could handle. I wanted to see the past, present and future all at the same time. I wanted to see the light side as much as the dark side. I wanted to see this reality, the space where we go when we die, other alien worlds, other galaxies, aliens and whatever else you can think up. I wanted to know how it all works. I wanted to see with my own eyes.

Remember, always only ask what you can handle.

It is because of this asking and its delivery that I am writing this book. What I am shown now calls for humanity to wake up. NOW.

Chapter 12

Get Your Affairs In Order

♥○♥

"I awoke, only to find that the rest of the world is still asleep."

Leonardo daVinci

Dying Again

While I have fast forwarded in my previous chapter, it is important to back track and fill you in on another dying episode of my life.

When my daughter was two and a half years old, we moved into our first home. It was December 15, 1995. All three of us got sick within two days of moving into the home, and although my husband and child recovered from the flu, I got sicker and sicker. Within eight weeks I had pneumonia and could barely stand up. I was barely able to crawl from the bedroom to the bathroom. My skin had leathery blotches all over my face and neck and at first it was believed that I had Lupus. When the test was negative I was sent to the infectious disease specialist who was sure I was dying of Lymphoma, cancer of the lymph nodes.

She said: *"It looks like you have six weeks to six months to live. I suggest you go home and make your last will. We should know more in a couple of days."*

Again!? Shit!

I asked her what else it could be if it wasn't Lymphoma and she said that whatever it was, I was dying. I could tell she had been at this for a long time, and I appreciated her candidness.

I remember driving home crying because this time I was not ready to die. I had a little two and a half year old girl and a husband to take care of. I wondered if all my praying for my life to end had finally caught up with me and I had finally gotten my wish. I was really sick and could not imagine continuing my life in this agonizing state. The physical pain was almost unbearable.

I realized that my daughter would not remember me when she grew up, I was thinking of leaving her letters or a video or pictures and I started a little diary for her. We had life insurance and it would be enough for my husband to pay off the mortgage and with his salary to live a good life while raising our daughter. He could remarry for love's sake but wasn't forced to remarry for money's sake. That felt good.

After crying for a couple of hours I was ready to let go. I did as the doctor suggested, typed up my last will and called our neighbors to sign on the dotted line. We didn't have much. I was just getting ready to turn 30 and our material belongings were simple to list.

As I laid on my bed with a body so broken and ready to let go of, I started to talk to God and I asked a lot of questions.

"Why now, God? All this time I had been wanting to be with you and now that I have finally made peace that this is my life for now and I have a child to raise, now you are calling me home? Was this it!? This was all I was supposed to accomplish? Was I supposed to give birth to this magnificent child and now my job is done? Really!?"

I didn't get an answer.

I laid there for a long time, feeling the inside workings of my body. I floated through my body watching my cells, I floated through my veins wondering where the culprit was. I couldn't find anything.

Suddenly the voice reappeared. The same voice that appeared to me when I was a little girl. The same voice that accompanied me through childhood. The same voice that called into my ears to get

up and rush to the hospital. There it was with yet another message:

"What if you were never one to begin with?"

The question was accompanied with dozens of visions lasting a split second, showing me chemical reactions that take place when hydrogen merges with oxygen, sodium with chloride, and so on. I was flashed before me the visions I had when I was frozen in amazement before the farm when I was a little girl. And I remembered my promise:

"I'm going to marry a farmer."

Suddenly I realized that as I floated around in my body and looked at my cells interacting, my husband's cells were not present inside my being. He was not my hydrogen! Source never had a chance to unite us because I was not his oxygen. I was his peroxide...

The promise *"and the two shall become one"* never applied.

This may sound funny to you, but it was all I needed to get an instant healing. I instantly knew that I was not dying of Lymphoma for as long as I heeded God's calling. I knew that I needed to find my farmer, and let go of the husband I had married.

Suddenly the three emergency surgeries made sense. It was the Universe flagging me down in an attempt to stop me from making a mistake. I didn't listen.

I promised to leave my husband when the time was right and to own up to my promise to *"love him until death do us part."* I had

the revelation of a lifetime. I didn't say *"I will live with you until death do us part, no matter how unhappy we both are."* I said *"I will love you and honor you and respect you until death do us part."* And that was a promise that I could still keep.

I felt instant liberation and a freedom I hadn't felt in so long!

I was just about thirty when this realization hit. I knew the test results would come back negative or with an alternative diagnosis and I knew that no matter what the diagnosis was, I now had the answer to my own healing. Out of love and respect for our daughter my plan was to stay in the marriage until she was an adult. My husband was a good man, he was loyal, honest, faithful, kind and in many ways a perfect guy. He just wasn't mine. He was occupying someone else's seat and I was occupying someone else's seat as well.

Unfortunately, my attempt to get my husband's agreement to divorce didn't go over so well. He didn't want to hear of a future divorce, he wanted to work hard to make it work. He deserved that, we deserved that. It would take another eight years of working hard, or shall I say, of squeezing a square peg into a round hole, before we both agreed that it was time to free up these sacred spaces next to us and give them to our rightful partners.

The diagnosis did come back negative for Lymphoma, now they started to look for other diseases such as Lupus, MS, Hepatitis and such, before getting the diagnosis of Fibromyalgia and Chronic Fatigue Immune Deficiency Disorder.

We parted as best friends. Our divorce cost less than $290 in filing fees and almost a decade later we remain great friends. The promise *"I love, respect and honor you until death do us part"* has

remained in tact for both of us. Not only for the sake of our daughter but for the sake of the promise we made.

The Real Tragedy of Divorce

What is so tragic about divorce is not the divorce itself but the damage it leaves behind once two people who once loved each other get through demolishing a once beautiful garden with their emotional bulldozers. What is so horrible about divorce is not the splitting up and moving on alone but it's the hatred that spews from one or both partners, the manipulations and the lies. Divorce is not bad, it's a blessing when two people can come to the table and honestly say that it is time to move on without each other but remain protective of their love and grateful and honorable for the love and time they did experience together.

Just a few weeks ago, nine years after our divorce, I was finally able to meet his fiancé and we simply hugged and I was able to extend my gratitude to her for taking such good care of my ex-husband and being such a great friend to our now adult daughter.

As my own spiritual unfolding has taken place and finding it so easy to 'see' people's internal workings on a cellular level, I find the majority of couples a complete mismatch. The true union on a chemical level never takes place and yet because of *Shoulditis* people stay in marriages and relationships by making their children or the finances the glue.

We don't have time to waste our precious souls on living with people who are not bringing forth our highest good. If you're in the wrong partnership, by all means love them enough to set them free. Love your children enough to be a good example for them by showing them that you are not staying in a non-

beneficial and non-productive marriage by sacrificing your own happiness, and theirs, to something that is bound to crumble anyways. Squeezing a square peg hurts not only you and your partner and your children, it hurts the planet because the energy you emanate is not one of unconditional love.

You want unconditional love? Lao Russell says it so beautifully: *"Love does not come to you from the horizon, it spreads from within you far beyond your horizon."*

♥O♥O♥O♥O♥O♥O♥O♥O♥O♥O♥O♥O♥O♥O♥O♥O♥O♥O♥O♥O♥O♥O♥O♥O♥O♥O♥O♥O♥O♥O♥

Chapter 13

Dismantling The Ego

♥○♥

"The ultimate lesson all of us have to learn is unconditional love, which includes not only others but ourselves as well."

Elisabeth Kuebler-Ross

Giving Life Over to Source

It was a Wednesday, the day before my 40th birthday. I had been a single mom for two years and I was doing great in every way. My health improved, and my daughter and I spent a lot of time together. After my divorce I took our daughter out of middle school and enrolled her in a high school program that would allow her to get herself through the rest of middle school and high school from the comfort of our home. I had started my own business teaching in-person workshops and tele-seminars and my schedule was so flexible that it allowed us to spend a lot of quality time together as mother and daughter. One of my wishes before having children was that I would be a stay-home mom from the time my children turn twelve. Twelve was when my Spirit started to disconnect and life became too burdensome for me. When I turned twelve my Dad left and my mother was working six days a week, twelve hour days, it seemed as though I never saw either of my parents after I turned twelve. I didn't want this kind of life for my daughter. This was my chance to build a great relationship with her as she was defining and redefining herself again and again as she was going through her teenage years. How blessed I was!

Suddenly I realized that history has a strange way of repeating itself. I wondered why my father left against our will when I was twelve and here was my daughter, the same age, without her father living in the same household. The situation, however, was completely different. My father left without a trace, without warning, without saying goodbye and without ever calling or making an effort to stay in touch. We on the other hand continued our weekly family dinners and we continued meeting for tea every other day to continue resolving the emotional aspects of our divorce. We knew that no matter how great our

relationship was, there was a mourning period to go through and there were many regrets, wounds, worries and things to talk about. Not having a chance to get these things resolved are the very things that end up tearing people apart in the end, causing for hatred to be born and fester and destroy the relationship. We didn't want it to be this way, we wanted peace. So we continued meeting for an entire year afterwards, every two to three days, to talk about our hurts and pains, to forgive and be forgiven, to laugh and to talk about our daughter.

The Biggest Decision of My Life

My life was going so good that no matter what I was going to do, I knew it would be blissful. I was happy and healthy and I was content being a single mom. I had no interest in dating, all I wanted was to be a great single mom, build my business and expand my soul through my spiritual journeys. I wanted to be about my highest purpose and was convinced that I was on the right track.

As I sat there on my bed looking over the beautiful San Francisco Bay with the East Bay glistening in the far distance and the beautiful Redwood trees and hills of Marin hugging the landscape in front of me, I asked God the question of a life time. It went something like this:

"God, I've had an amazing life so far. I've experienced so many brushes with death, have been so ill and experienced so much health and happiness in my body, I've been married and now am enjoying my life as a single mother, I've made a good living working part time and I am living the dream of being a stay-home mom to my wonderful daughter. I am deeply grateful for having had the steering wheel for all these years. I am half way through my physical

life and I would like to move over to the passenger seat so you can take over the driver's seat. You drive, you guide, you decide where we go. You live through me, move the 'me' that I think I am out of the way and occupy my body so you can experience the greatest life possible through this physical body."

WARNING!

Dear reader, I must give you a legal disclaimer. Do not, absolutely do not pray this prayer unless you are truly ready to get your "I" dismantled or the "I" that you think you are. Source wants nothing more than to live and have its experience through you. We live little lives compared to the big lives we could actually live. We live our lives with our intellect, which is a tiny, tiny aspect of this physical reality and is not related to the unseen world at all. Our little ego's entire purpose is to keep our physical vessel alive and to do so at all cost. Our real purpose, however, can only reveal itself once we let go of our intellect, our little ego and the plan and desires we cling to for dear life.

In order for Source to have its being and movement through you, however, it needs to first clean the heart drive and do a complete uninstall of the programs we have allowed to be installed by our little ego, our belief systems and our intellect, this includes programs that have been installed by mass entrainment, the media, the government, our tribe and family members, friends and co-workers and programs that have been installed by extra-terrestrials.

This is the most serious heart drive swipe you can possibly pray for. Do not pray for such a clean-swipe unless you are truly ready to let go of everything and everyone. I had no idea what I was asking for. I am only now, many years later, with hindsight on one

side and linear time on my other side, in a position to see what I really asked for was quite irresponsible.

Finally - She's Ready!

It was as if the entire heavenly realm was assembling and exclaiming:

"Finally! She is ready!"

And in came the sweeper teams and cleared me of just about everything that I owned and thought I owned. I learned very quickly that we own absolutely nothing in this life, not even our bodies. Within less than six months I had lost friends, all of my assets, my clients, my entire business and my health was failing once again.

And there was the voice again but this time not with a message of encouragement but instructions:

"Become celibate."
"Stop eating."
"Do not associate with groups."
"Do not read any books."

"This is my mission!? What! Do you want me to go to Nepal and live naked in some cave?" I asked loaded with cynicism.

I didn't get an answer. I never do when I ask with a cynical undertone.

I learned a long time ago that asking Spirit 'why' questions rarely get answered. The 'why' is rarely important. What is important is the faith by which I carry out my new instructions.

Was I tempted to take back my request to have Source live through me? You bet I did! I cried myself to sleep many nights wondering whatever got into my head asking for Source to take over my life. Who was God anyway? Was he really to be trusted? Was he not just a figment of the imagination of those who painted some white guy with a beard sitting somewhere on a white cloud with a black whip waiting for us to fail just so he could punish us?

I remembered the story of Job. No, I would not be like Job. I knew better to insult the incomprehensible, static, white light that 'just is,' penetrating all, resting in everything and having its being through all that lives. And yet Source is none of those things. I knew better.

I went out on faith no matter how far I needed to fall.

♥O♥O♥O♥O♥O♥O♥O♥O♥O♥O♥O♥O♥O♥O♥O♥O♥O♥O♥O♥O♥O♥O♥O♥O♥O♥O♥O♥O♥

Chapter 14

Who Are Your Spirit Guides?

♥O♥O♥O♥O♥O♥O♥O♥O♥O♥O♥O♥O♥O♥O♥O♥O♥O♥O♥O♥O♥O♥O♥O♥O♥O♥O♥O♥O♥O♥O♥O♥O♥O♥O♥

"Love does not come to you from the horizon, love spreads from within you far beyond your horizon."

Lao Russell

Which Side Is Talking?

One of the questions I get a lot from my coaching clients and forum members is "how to decipher if the spiritual message you receive is from the light or dark side."

This is probably one of the greatest questions ever because the dark side's best skill is masquerading as angels of the light. As many near death experiences as I have had and seeing dark beings as well as light beings, they still tried to sneak into an assembly by dressing up as light beings. If you get one thing about this topic it must be this:

They must tell the truth. No exception.

They can show up as an angel of light, deceive you, manipulated you, take your health from you, even harvest your soul from you when you shed your body, but what they can't do is lie. And in order for you to figure out who is there in the privacy of your own spiritual gatherings, it is of utmost importance that you ask if they are all of the light. Those who are not must show themselves. And then you can ask them to be transmuted into light or ask them to be escorted away to where they came from.

Here is another example.

A woman I once knew had absolutely amazing insights from the spirit world and while much of her messages were 'right on,' many of them came from the completely wrong source. For example, she tried to convince me that Spirit will stoop as low as to lie to us if it meant for us to do something it wants us to do.

Never, ever, does Spirit interfere with our own free will. and lying to us to get what it wants is just not how our light Source operates.

Use your head. If this spirit or voice asks you to do something that would hurt you or someone else, you are not listing to Source but some other source of dark energies.

Spirit never yells, screams, curses or puts you down, ever. And it will never ask you to harm anything or anyone.

The Spirit of Source is neither male or female. If you hear a male or female voice you are dealing with a deceased person, dark entity or an alien energy. Even the lowest of light angels are neutral and generally neither male nor female. Yes, we define Archangel Michael as male, however, he isn't and when you have the true Archangel Michael with you, you will know this. If you can clearly hear a male Archangel Michael ask which side he serves. Remember, even our Archangels have a dark counter part, as does everything in the seen and unseen world. In other words, for every heavenly angel there is an angel matching its vibration on the shadow side.

Another hint is that the Spirit of Source rarely, if ever, repeats their instructions. The instructions usually come in a very calm, soft voice and they are transmitted telepathically for the most part, if not always.

Above all remember that Source is pure, unconditional love and therefore patient always. If your Spirit guide is impatient or shows any human emotions at all, you are not dealing with the Spirit of Source. If the message you are given is not loving towards you or your fellow beings, then you are listening to the

wrong voices. You are always allowed free will and Spirit will always honor this precious gift.

To get help with this most important task of expanding your own intuition, consider joining our spiritual forum and get insights from others who are on the same journey. We even have a **Practice Your Intuition** forum where you can practice your intuitive gifts and give and receive readings as well as dream analysis.

You can find us here: www.CoreFreedom.com

♥O♥O♥O♥O♥O♥O♥O♥O♥O♥O♥O♥O♥O♥O♥O♥O♥O♥O♥O♥O♥O♥O♥O♥O♥O♥O♥O♥O♥O♥O♥

Chapter 15

Karma vs. Cause and Effect

♥0♥0♥0♥0♥0♥0♥0♥0♥0♥0♥0♥0♥0♥0♥0♥0♥0♥0♥0♥0♥0♥0♥0♥0♥0♥0♥0♥0♥0♥0♥0♥

"A man who fears suffering is already suffering from what he fears."

Michel de Montaigne

Karma versus Cause and Effect

One of the most misunderstood and mixed up principles are those of karma and cause and effect. Many teach and think that karma is cause and effect. The entire Eastern spiritual philosophies are based on this one law: karma.

Karma is not Cause and Effect. On the contrary.

In simple terms, karma has been known as 'what goes around comes around,' similarly to the boomerang effect.

Karma teaches us that we are basically screwed, whether we do it this way or that way, it's a lose-lose situation and no matter what we do, we will pay for whatever choice we make.

Karma is not only 100% human created but it leaves us powerless and it highly favors some and not others. Above all, karma instills fear whereas the law of cause and effect teaches us to think and then make choices. Karma also teaches us that we are bound by a law *outside* of us and therefore we do not need to take responsibility for ourselves, therefore many conclude that thinking is futile because we're not going to win anyways. With Karma we remain victims.

The law of Cause and Effect is never-changing and has nothing to do with human failure or human punishment. The law of Cause and Effect is solid, steady, never-changing and does not favor anyone. That's why it is said that God is just.

It has been said that the man or woman who knows "cause" knows everything. How true!

We use the terms 'karma' and 'cause and effect' interchangeably and I urge you to become aware that although they look similar, they are worlds apart. Karma is man-made and the ultimate fear inducing threat to any and all of us. It is a bigger fear inducing threat than the threat of 'heaven or hell.' Karma leaves us defeated because we can't win either way. What's worse is that 'karma' supposedly penetrates all time and space. So we live life wondering if our 'bad luck' is due to all the evil we have caused in our previous life times. Living based on karma is the ultimate experienced of being chained to a dungeon created by our own minds. The entrainment of believing in this faulty, man-made, non-existent, false 'law' causes us to feel defeated, depleted and unmotivated.

The law of Cause and Effect, however, is based on solid, natural laws and does not play favoritism. The way to work with the law of Cause and Effect is to utilize your gifts of thinking and free will. The only Universal law you need to learn and understand is the law of Cause and Effect. All other Universal laws are merely effects of this basic law, which is the basic law of the interchange between all opposites that exist.

You don't even have to learn about the law of attraction as the law of attraction is a horizontal law to you, whereas the law of gravity is a vertical law to you. In other words, everything that goes up must come down - this is the basic law of gravity. No one questions this fact. Similarly, the law of attraction attracts to you everything which emanates out from within you. In essence, the law of attraction is the exact same law as the law of gravity.

What controls both the law of gravity and the law of abundance is the law of Cause and Effect. And the brilliant part is that you can create, i.e. cause anything you want. And yes, you must take

personal responsibility for your choices. That's living a co-created life.

What you must remember and what most people forget, is that 'cause and effect' permeate time and space as well. We cannot possibly believe that whatever we do in this life is ending the moment your souls slips off its body suit. Time and space in reality do not exist. What we call life and death are just rhythms that appear like 'life' and later appear like 'death.' Both are life - one where you can be seen in this realm and the other where you cannot be seen in this realm.

Whatever you do to your body or to your life or someone else's life you will re-live because for every action there is a reaction, both in this realm as well as in the unseen realm. In other words, if you mistreat your body in this life and you destroy your body to an early refolding, don't expect to get the body featuring perfect health in your next life. What you do now will have an effect, sometimes the effect is visible immediately, other times the effect takes a much longer time (life times) to become visible.

Everything you put out has its duplicate action in the unseen realm and you will relive your output once again. Otherwise, how else can you soul take inventory of where it still has lessons to learn?

That's why we are gifted with the faculties called *thinking* and *making choices*, two abilities excessively under-utilized by the human population.

Now let me get back to tell you what happened once Source dismantled my beautiful life.

Chapter 16

New Assignments - Rebirth

♥○♥

"People are like stained-glass windows. They sparkle and shine when the sun is out, but when the darkness sets in, their true beauty is revealed only if there is a light from within."

Elisabeth Kuebler-Ross

My New Assignments - My New Life

I was mad at God, yes, but getting mad at God is futile. I was more mad at myself for asking God to move into the driver seat. What was I ever thinking!?

I had no interest in acquiring a new life, my life was just dandy, fine and successful the way it was. But praying for Source to take over your life is bound to rock any foundation to the ground. I felt much like Job who lost everything, including his children, all but his nagging wife. His faith was seriously tested. At least I had my health and my daughter, but not for long. My health soon after began to fail once again and my daughter turned into a person I barely recognized. *"Was she really my daughter?"* I asked myself often.

I soon realized that I had been asked to take up my own cross and walk a path to my own crucifixion. I remembered Solomon's proverb: **"Only a fool makes promises he can't keep."** I had promised to let God drive, there was no turning back and I did not know what my resurrection looked like, I just knew that the path was one of silence and solitude.

Celibacy

I had been single for a few years and the instructions to become celibate were not so unbearable for me as they might be to some. I had always been a one-man kind of woman; what concerned me just a little bit was that I was not given a deadline of any sorts. I knew that once I vowed to celibacy that it would be according to God's terms, not mine. I would have to be willing to live this life

style until the day I died, unless Source had other plans for me. I asked for more details but wasn't given any.

Source often does this because with everything we must be in it with all of our hearts, minds and soul and not according to our terms. This is where humanity is making the biggest mistakes. We want to paint God the way we want him to be. And of course this means that we get everything exactly the way we want it, when we want it and we want it all yesterday. Source doesn't work this way, hence why the human drama. This was my opportunity to really get to know God and to let 'him' show me who 'he' was, rather than me coming up with my own limited version of what this power might be all about. I went out on faith.

I was concerned that I would not have what it takes to stay true to my promise. So I asked for help. Getting on my knees I asked for assistance so that if this was truly what I needed to do to have Source live through me, that I would be willing to live such a life style. I asked for Spirit's support.

Suddenly a swoosh of wind came through the room and through my body. There was no window open and it literally felt like a draft came through the room. I felt the draft penetrate my every cell, it went straight through my body and suddenly I was enveloped by the same energy that I felt as a little girl standing before the farm. I heard Spirit whisper that *"this was the energy I needed to wait for and that it would reveal itself in due time."*

Even though I was already on my knees I felt like I wanted to dissolve into nothingness, I felt exactly like I did in the tunnel the moment I heard the most amazing angel voices humming their tune of unconditional love.

I knew enough about Spirit to know that in the unseen world time and space don't exist. So while "due time" could mean one year, ten years or twenty life times, this was not up to me to control and I needed to trust and have faith that 'due time' meant 'due time' in Spirit's language, however long that would be.

I cried out of reverence for this energy enveloping me. And for the first time I felt as though the energy had a hint of masculinity with it. In other words, when I was a little girl I simply felt a powerful energy, I couldn't tell if it was male or female. This time, however, it felt as though this was my true life partner's energy. I knew I needed to be faithful to this energy, not only for his sake but for the world's sake.

This experience was loaded with visions from Spirit that showed me the world's state of being, the sadness, the longing for this type of oneness and the desperation and thirst of people's souls trying to live lives of bliss. Humanity was so wrapped up in the sensed world, constantly trying to please and satisfy yet another one of their senses, that they never sat long enough, still enough, to hear their souls' longings.

Seeing into the hearts of so many human beings I was overcome with sadness and knew that being celibate for the sake of the planet would be an easy task.

All desire left my body. Something changed. As a symbol of reclaiming my second virginity and dedication to Source I placed a belly chain around my second chakra with two symbolic pendants, one in the front and one in the back. I felt as though I had gotten married to God.

As soon as I left the house something had changed in the way I saw people. Suddenly I saw their souls hovering in their 8th or

9th chakra area, connected to their 7th chakra with a silver cord, and yet no one was really listening to their souls. It was as if their pour souls were just hostages tied to physical bodies that were dominated by computer programs that seemed to run their physical bodies with ego, senses, lust, gluttony and the intellect.

Men didn't look like men anymore, they looked like beautiful Beings who were here to experience a rich life. Women didn't look like women anymore, they looked just as magnificent - beings who were here to experience their souls' longings to the fullest. Sometimes when I walk behind couples I can't tell the difference between the man and the woman, they are just beautiful spirits to me.

Men suddenly didn't look handsome or cute anymore. The feeling or desire to be in a relationship suddenly disappeared. At first I welcomed the detachment, years later I started to worry that I was 'defective' in some way. I had to constantly remind myself that I had received a heart drive clean-sweep and somehow this part of my program was no longer installed.

Groups, Tribes and Reading Books

This was by far the easiest task for me to accomplish. A hermit and shy by nature anyways these were welcoming instructions. I had spent most of my childhood alone, either in my room, in the forest or on the farm. Not associating with people or participating in workshops sounded like a great idea. But I didn't know why and I really wanted to know why this was so important to Source.

I soon got my answer.

To assist me with this task I was asked to move out of the United States and into the Northern Italian mountains and then the Swiss Alps to spend time alone. A couple of years later I was guided to move to Sedona, back in the United States, where I would need to spend most of my time hiking barefoot in the red mountains of Sedona.

It wasn't until six years of solitude and much expansion later that I was realizing and understanding the impact of true solitude and celibacy. It had to do with entrainment and not being a part of the mass consciousness. While mass consciousness is always affecting us, even the loneliest, most secluded sages in Himalayan caves are affected by our mass consciousness. Entrainment, however, has a completely different, much more powerful impact on our human mind than anything else.

Albert Einstein said it best: *"The one who follows the crowd will usually get no further than the crowd. The one who walks alone, is likely to find himself in places no one has ever been."*

If there is only one more thing you remember from this book then I would like it to be this:

Whoever controls your mind controls your soul.

When you are born you are born into a tribe. Your tribe not only consists of your family, it consists of the country that you are born in. If you are born in the United States, then the collective mind of the U.S. will have an effect on you, no matter where you are in the world and no matter whether you have renounced your American citizenship or not. Even if you were off living a blissful life on another continent, whatever happens to the United States has a most immediate and powerful affect on your DNA.

Add to that the impact and programming of our day-to-day habits, such as radio and TV shows, magazines and newspapers you read, places you hang out in and so on.

Living in solitude and away from the crowed, while being celibate for five years has taught me the real meaning and purpose of detachment. Without having experienced such detachment one cannot even begin to comprehend the power of these outside forces that we are continually subjected to.

I am not at all saying that you need to become celibate. This was my journey. Remember, even three near-death experience didn't wake me up. I needed to get banged over the head some more. This book is hopefully helping expand some of your consciousness so you don't have to go through the head-banging class at the University of hard-knocks.

Spirit needed to show me something, teach me something. And I wouldn't trade a day of this lesson. And just perhaps my telling you about my experience is sufficient so you don't have to go through the experience yourself.

When it comes to sexuality, what I do urge people to learn and fully understand is the difference between sense oriented sexuality and sacred sexuality. One is life giving in the unseen realms and the other is life reducing in the unseen (and seen) realms. I have written several chapters about sacred sexuality in my book, **Quantum Love**, which is available here as an eBook.

http://www.corefreedom.com/resources/quantum-love-divine-relationships-myth-or-reality.3/

Partnering With Your Divine Partner

In my book, **Quantum Love: Divine Relationship**, I talk in much detail about the holiness and sacredness of divine relationships and the difference between 'regular' relationships, which are mainly karmic in nature, and divine relationships that have a much more significant purpose here on this planet. Not everyone believes in a divinely assigned partner and that is the way it is supposed to be. Only you know if this calling is within you. If it is, it is there because you are meant to find him or her, so that together you can unfold your purpose here for humanity. The planet is desperate for sacred relationships that serve as a new foundation and example to a new world that is desperately longing for new hope of a love that is so unconditional that it can only come from Source.

Yes, we can create a good or even a great marriage with just about anyone. After all, I was in such a marriage. And Rumi is very right when he says that *"your task is not to seek for love, but merely to seek and find all the barriers with yourself that you have built against it."*

So yes, your first job is to remove those barriers and once again realize love indeed does not come to you from far away but that true, unconditional love spreads from within you far beyond your horizon.

There comes a time in someone's journey where living out karmic lives with soul mates is no longer satisfactory and if you are a spiritually advanced person you know how to work through 'karma' or past life memories with people on a platonic level, rather than marrying the person and for three decades hammering them into a mold they will simply never fit into. This is just insanity and yet this is exactly what so many do.

I have created many videos on sacred sexuality, which can be found on my YouTube channel, BlueprintforLove. You will find the links in the Resources section. If you are truly ready to take your sexuality to a sacred level, then the book, **Quantum Love: Divine Relationships**, contains close to a hundred pages on just sacred sexuality.

If you feel the call, it is now time to clear your space for this rightful partner of yours to step in and reunite with you so that together you can help lift the planet's vibration.

My Next Assignment - Living Without Food

This is the topic I will speak the least about because it is the least understood and therefore also the most dangerous journey to embark on. It is also the topic that invokes the most fear in people and there is no reason to go there. Let me share just a little bit of this journey with you.

When I first heard the message that I need to stop eating food I threw a serious fit and went straight into a panic. Didn't God remember that I went to bed without food when I was a little girl? What, now I was supposed to purposely starve myself to death!? Was this a joke?

I just couldn't wrap my head around this ridiculous task and thought not eating would surely kill me. I was convinced that this was the dumbest and most stupid thing anyone could ever do! After all, didn't we have taste buds, teeth, a stomach and an excretory system for a reason? Was I really listening to Spirit or was this some other program that slipped into my heart drive to throw me into confusion?

This was a serious hurdle for me, one I was not sure I wanted to even take on. In fact, if you are reading this I am urging you to <u>not</u> embark on this journey. The line between not eating and starvation looks almost identical. I read that over 115 million children under the age of 5 die every year of hunger. What would be different for me? Was God seriously kidding me!?

The only difference between breatharianism and starvation is awareness and consciousness. That's it. And consciousness is not just awareness within the mind, it is full awareness within the seven-nervous centers and on a DNA and cellular level. It's a calling, not an idea or plan to be under taken by the intellect because science and the ego will never be able to wrap their data around God. The facts of millions of people starving every year, however, is a reality of this domain. Heed it.

As with most of my assigned tasks, I gave Spirit the right of passage. I had given my life over to God the day before I turned forty. I had no intentions of turning back now. But I had serious work to do just to wrap my head around this insane path. I asked for help.

Did I already tell you about the magic of asking and then simply receiving?

I expressed my sincerest desire to want to do what is in my highest good and for the highest good of life everywhere. I confessed my intense fear around this task and asked for assistance and some time.

Well, time is not something Spirit is very good at once a life has been given over to Source. You see, the Universe loves, absolutely loves speed! I have learned that when I am stepping out of the way and allow the divine spark of my soul to lay before

me all things possible, the Universe manifests often almost immediately.

And this was no different.

It was a Friday and I came down with the stomach flu. *"Great,"* I thought to myself, *"first my daughter, now me."* I didn't think anything of the excessive vomiting and the intense pain. But when I found myself stand in the medicine isle on the third day with a bottle of laxative in my hands because I still had not been able to go to the bathroom, I heard the voice loud and clear:

"Don't!"

I had enough trust in my higher guidance than to disobey this urging no matter how much I felt like I needed to use the bathroom. And I'm glad I did. I went back home, went back to bed and got sicker and sicker. On the fourth day at two in the morning I tried making my way back from the bathroom to my bedroom. I wanted to vomit but there was nothing left to vomit. I was completely dehydrated.

There was a thud and I collapsed on the kitchen floor. My daughter heard the fall and called the ambulance. By the time I got to the hospital I had pneumonia and was not expected to live. My appendix had ruptured four days before. People often ask me if it didn't hurt and I often tell them that yes, it did. But with so many surgeries, giving birth and the fact that my daughter had just finished her stomach flu the day before me, I simply thought I had a bad case of stomach flu.

Yes, I had re-enrolled for another class at the University of hard-knocks.

I was in the hospital for a long time and unable to get any visitors. I wasn't even allowed to get phone calls. I often saw the world twirl in the periphery of my eyes. The all-too-familiar twirls that so gently signaled that life as I knew it was about to end. And yet there was no thought or worry of not making it. Somehow it never crossed my mind, even though the hospital staff checked on me every twenty minutes around the clock.

By the time I left the hospital I had lost 16 pounds in less than 10 days, and the thought of food was nauseating to me.

Although I tried to recover from this incident, I got sicker and sicker. I contracted one immune deficiency after another and the thought of food became simply repulsive to me.

♥O♥O♥O♥O♥O♥O♥O♥O♥O♥O♥O♥O♥O♥O♥O♥O♥O♥O♥O♥O♥O♥O♥O♥O♥O♥O♥O♥

Again!?

Nine months after my ruptured appendix, I had gotten so sick that I found myself getting diagnosed with pneumonia a chronic ear infection and asthma. The coughing and vomiting up to ten times a day became unbearable. It got so bad that I couldn't even leave the house as I would start vomiting in the most inconvenient places, such as the grocery store.

One day I woke up with the right side of my face completely drooping. My right eye was almost completely closed and I was unable to pull up my right eye brow. Feeling no pain other than from the constant coughing and feeling as if my face had gotten a shot from the dentist, my frightened neighbor begged me to call the emergency room to get checked for a stroke immediately.

I felt fine, what was she talking about?

Clearly, however, my face looked awfully distorted and something was not right. I went to see a neurologist right away and was sent to the hospital immediately for an MRI. He said to him it looked like I either had a stroke or an aneurysm and they wanted to see how bad it was.

What!? Not again!

The MRI came back negative. He had four other neurologists come in and look at my MRI. No stroke, no aneurysm in the head. Only four puzzled neurologists. A thorough eye exam proved my right optic nerve to be pinched or torn and I was diagnosed with Horner's Syndrome. Something was causing pressure on the optic nerve, but what? Since I tested negative for Bells Palsy, he was sure that with my history of frequent pneumonias that there must be a tumor either on my thymus gland or in my lungs, which was pushing on my optic nerve.

Great - here we go looking for reasons why my body seemingly wanted to check out once again.

"But I'm not ready now, God!" I complained. *"Why now when I'm finally starting to figure out this life of mine!?"*

There was no answer.

My vision in my right eye dramatically decreased and in just a few days I could barely see with my right eye, everything seemed to glisten, move and appear multiple times. Very annoying.

And yet test after test revealed that I did not have pneumonia, no middle ear infection and no asthma and yet even though putting

cocaine in my eyes proved that I test 100% positive for Horner's Syndrome, they simply could not find the darn tumor that seems to be pushing on this optic nerve.

Every time they asked me for other symptoms besides the numbness in my face, the coughing, the closed eye and inability to see, I kept telling them that I felt as though I had intense pressure on the right side of my head and an abnormal amount of fluid behind my right eye, I could feel it when I laid on my right side and it hurt my right ear and I kept coughing and coughing. All tests just showed weird results, even the doctors were puzzled.

I was mad at the doctors for putting me through one test after another, finding absolutely nothing concrete. And mad at God for being so vague about what was really going on.

I noticed that eating made my coughing worse and coughing made my eye worse and increased fluid in my head and lungs.

Suddenly one day I remembered that the instructions several years ago were to stop eating. It became clear that this was Spirit's way of helping me along. After all, I did ask Spirit to help. I was tired of the physical suffering, I had nothing to lose. *"I might as well do this Spirit's way,"* I thought to myself.

My biggest obstacle in this journey was not my body getting used to not eating, it was the training of the ego and the reprogramming of the oh-so powerful mind that was not going to have any part in this journey.

Adyashanti said that **"Enlightenment is the complete eradication of everything we imagined to be true."** This was my opportunity to learn that food was not a necessity for me, that in fact it was just an unnecessary burden to where my journey was headed.

I knew that this was one journey I could not take on with my intellect, this was a journey exclusively for Spirit. I realized full well that this was my opportunity to fully trust God and I was reminded by Bruce Lee's quote: **"The usefulness of the cup is its emptiness."** How right he was.

An egg can be cracked from the outside and so be destroyed, or we can crack it from within and so give birth to a new *reality*. It was a painful process and I often felt my cross was just too heavy to carry.

Even though I had already gotten the instructions from Spirit to embark on this journey, I consulted the I-Ching and the message couldn't have been clearer: **God is your bread.**

I remembered Rumi's quote: **"Your body is woven from the light of heaven"** and no matter how many times doubt crept in, I knew I would be just fine.

It took me years of mental work and of changing my diet from vegetarian to vegan, to raw food, to fresh veggie juices to fruits to fruit juices and a handful of seeds per day. The mental work by far was the most difficult challenge I have ever undertaken. The social implications and the restrictions this life style would cause me were often overwhelming.

Before I was even ready to embark on this journey I knew I needed to first face and then master my fear of starvation. Although I never had an eating disorder, I was always well prepared by having food in the house. I lived by the rule of *"just in case there is a shortage one day."* I had to learn to face this fear. And I did.

Meanwhile I was called to move to Sedona where I knew my final switch would take place. I asked the infamous 'why' question and was surprised to be given vision after vision. When I first was given these instructions I wasn't shown how long I would have to go without food and for what purpose exactly. Here I was and suddenly I was flooded with visions of worldwide food poisoning, shortages of food and the appearance of viruses that would easily kill people unless their systems were as clear as possible. I was not given any dates and times and I rarely focus on the dates of my visions because they are forever changing. What I do trust is that the instructions from Source are always right on. Whether they are right on for all the world or just me is a different story.

When I asked why I was not to eat but the rest of the world was not required to abstain from food I was shown that it was not necessary for the rest of the world to learn to live on just air and water. I was not shown if this path was for personal reasons or to somehow help people in the future with a similar path, perhaps when we are forced to live on less as a society. I really don't know and I am not attached to outcomes.

Learning how not to eat and trust Source completely and fully was by far the most challenging and difficult journey I have ever taken on. Suddenly the time came when I found myself not having eaten in three months and by this time I had not had any water for eight days but was still hiking for two to three hours per day, barefoot. How was this even humanly possible?

It's simple. It's not.

This was the whole purpose of me learning this lesson. Here I found myself empty of all that I thought constituted of the "I" that I had been identifying with for so many years. And yet here I was having no sensed experiences beyond hiking barefoot. Living

celibate for over five years, with a body that was sustained with something other than food, participating in no workshops, spending time with almost no one. My mind was sharper than ever before, my body was healthier than ever before and I was seemingly floating across the red Sedona sand. Jumping off rocks was a brand new learning experience, it was as if I had to learn to inhabit this physical vessel once again.

And the visions started to flood in.

Earth Changes

Visions of massive earth changes ahead. Visions of loss of human lives, visions of an entire galactic gathering for the upcoming events. When I look at the Universe or the space 'out there' beyond our planet, we have Beings visiting and assembling for these great events, I couldn't even begin to give you the details. Some are here to assist, others are here to destroy, others are here to rebuild, everyone has a purpose.

And meanwhile, humanity is fast sleep, chasing after the next meal, the next skirt, the next paycheck, the next materialistic gadget, all while completely missing the point. Even those that are consumed with the banking scandal and the conspiracies and GMO foods are missing the point, by a long shot. If you could only see how unimportant and menial all of these things are compared to the bigger picture that is about to unfold before us. All of these things are here to distract you. These distractions have been planted and are computer programs that are here to keep you away from seeing, hearing and knowing what is really going on.

It's wake up time! NOW!

Meanwhile, other Beings I call Snatchers are waiting to harvest human souls during the great transition of the masses. The unsuspecting souls that the world now calls sheeple, who are sheeple not only in this realm, but remain asleep when shedding their bodies. These are the easiest souls to snatch, which is what all of this hoopla is about.

This is not a book about telling you about my near death experiences, this is a book about getting the spark within your own soul woken once again so you can wake up and remember that life not a fraction as important as the evolution and salvation of your soul. And right now the majority of our human souls are in real danger. And the only person who can do anything about it is you. You must wake up. Now.

In the next chapter let me share with you the most important message that you may ever get in your life...

♥0♥0♥0♥0♥0♥0♥0♥0♥0♥0♥0♥0♥0♥0♥0♥0♥0♥0♥0♥0♥0♥0♥0♥0♥0♥0♥0♥0♥0♥

Chapter 17

The Fabric of Our Soul

♥○♥

"When you lose all sense of self the bonds of a thousands chains will vanish. Lose yourself completely, return to the root of the root of your own soul."

Rumi

The Fabric of Our Soul

It's a weekday and a perfect time to go to one of my all time favorite spots close to Muir Woods in Marin County, California. This specific spot has been one of my secret hide out places to rejuvenate, write, to do some quality thinking and find time to be alone with Source.

I had just finished writing in my diary when my entry had caused many questions about the fabric of our soul. People talk about spirit, soul, essence, light - where exactly is this soul housed within us?

I had seen the beautiful light that human beings really are, the electric field of their magnificence, but I knew what I had seen was not the actual soul. What I saw was just the spirit of our soul, but not the actual soul. I was ready to see the soul.

Feeling prompted to lay lengthwise on the wooden picnic table I closed my eyes and asked God to show me our soul's true magnificence.

With my eyes closed I suddenly saw something float above me that I had never seen before. It looked like a transparent egg without the shell and much larger; about 2 feet wide and deep by about 4-5 feet high. It had a pearl white type of mistiness to its outside membrane and a yolk within that contained the most brilliant shades of green, blue and violets. I had never seen such brilliance!

The colors within the yolk were dancing and creating the most amazing geometric formations, they were switching from waved patterns to the most intricate designs. The white, glowing

membrane on the outside was emitting the most amazing golden, white light. And everything was pulsating.

Out of this formation came the most angelic sound that reminded me of the sound in the tunnel when I had died the second time. There was music or humming coming from within this 'egg!' How brilliant! It was a sound that is not of this earth and I find no words to describe this beauty.

It beckoned me to come play. Strange! It communicated and I actually understood what it was saying. I was fascinated. There was a feeling of innocence and purity coming from within this 'egg' and I felt completely safe.

Suddenly I saw a second 'egg' formation to the left, only this one belonged to me. Without a doubt I knew that this was me because I now was looking from the body on the table at myself but at the same time I looked from this orange 'egg' down onto my body laying on the wooden bench.

The colors on the outside stayed the same as the other 'egg' but the content of the yolk were bright, rich bronze, orange, gold, yellows and some reds. I was watching the entire scene with my inner eye while laying on the table, with my eyes closed.

I had had out of body experiences before but this I had never experienced. At first I had no idea what I was looking at. I felt so much peace and so much joy and love being in the presence of this other being.

I quickly realized that he was leading the way. Off we flew faster than lightning speed we floated over the Pacific down to New Zealand. We combed through the mountains and floated across the ocean water when suddenly we collided into one, which

caused a sort of light collision, every illuminated around us, right before we dove into the ocean. Underneath the water as one 'egg' our center turned into the most beautiful rainbow colored display of heaven. There are not seven colors in the rainbow, there are so many more and here I saw the interchanging display of this union before my eyes. I was awestruck.

As we came back above water we separated only to collide again and again, creating one mini big bang after another. We experienced true soulgasms again and again. The joy and bliss and elation we felt is not an emotion that can even be described with our limited alphabet, in fact I wonder if such emotions are even existent on this plane.

We traveled through the world over many mountains and across many landscapes, collided and dove into oceans, separated again and on and on we played in a completely timeless experience.

It was time to return to my body. I didn't want to. I did not know who this other Being was other than that he was me also. My counter part. The music we created when our souls collided was heavenly, nothing human ears could ever fathom hearing. We must open our inner ears to hear such perfection, such beauty.

Back on site while hovering over my body I turned to my other, green, blue shimmering and very happy soul and he explained that he would one day find me again.

Off he floated away like a spaceship taking off at high speeds and I slipped back in my body.

When I came to it felt as though only 2-3 minutes must have past. My keys, wallet, pen and paper were still laying next to me. Invigorated I made my way back to my car when I realized that

four hours had past. How could this be!? How could my body lay there on a wooden picnic bench for four hours without anyone coming to ask if I was okay or even be tempted to take my things? I was on a divine journey and perhaps a divine bubble was around my body so no one even saw me there.

This happened many years ago and I have come to the resolve that our souls are more magnificent than anything we could ever explain. Some may say the soul is an essence, a light. It doesn't matter what description we give it. What's important is that we remember that our soul's evolution is all that matters. We must guard our soul and remember to pray for people's souls.

♥♡♥

Chapter 18

Four Doors

♥◊♥

"Be Content with what you have; rejoice in the way things are. When you realize there is nothing lacking, the whole world belongs to you."

Lao Tzu

The Four Doors of Life

My Mayan Astrologer gave me one of the most important lessons ever.

"There are four doors in life, through which ever man and woman must go through," he said.

He continued: "They are the door of fears, the door of clarity, the door of power and the door of wisdom."

"Everyone wants power and everyone wants clarity but almost no one wants to face their fears. And wisdom is last on anyone's list, people are more interested in intellectual knowledge than elder wisdom," he continued sharing.

He goes on: "Everyone wants to know where is the love of my life, what is my purpose, when will I own my own house, what's wrong with my health - everyone wants clarity! But no one understands that unless they have first walked through the door of fears the door of clarity cannot be opened for them."

"And the very few people who are willing to face their fears are unwilling to master their fears. Facing one's fears is not enough. We must master our fears. Only when we have mastered our fears will we be led to the door of clarity. And once we are clear about life, who we are, what we are here to do, we will be shown the door of true power. And only this true power, which comes from within, will lead to elder wisdom," he explained.

He continues: "What happens for most people, we see this often in positions of power, that people are very clear in what they want and they go straight to the door of power. But it's a false power

and it's a false sense of clarity. It is not the door of clarity or the door of power as provided by our God. Therefore, these people remain afraid deep down because they never deal with their fears, let alone master them. And little do they know that they will never achieve elder wisdom. All they achieve is useless degrees and intellectual knowledge but inside they remain dead, powerless and afraid."

I knew I had to go back in time and pull up all of my experiences and walk with them through my door of fears. My fear of starving to death, of being left in the forest, my fear of never amounting to anything as was repeatedly drilled into my little head, the fear of seeing so many men, women and children being victimized on a constant basis by misguided men, my fear of public speaking, because this meant I needed to show up naked, vulnerable on a soul level, and I didn't feel worthy. I would have rather died than spoken even at a friend's bridal or baby shower, that's how much I disliked speaking in front of groups. Fears, all fears!

It was time to not only face these fears, it was time to master them, one by one.

I remembered a scripture that said to "overcome evil with good." I looked at my fears as evil and I wanted to overcome them with good, their opposites. And one by one I turned every one of my fears into a beautiful gift.

One of my challenging and yet easiest ones to master was the fear of seeing so many victimized in my inner eyes. No matter if or how I would overcome this fear, the abuse would continue. I wondered "how can I possibly make a difference?"

One day I watched a Bollywood movie and within the first 10 seconds of the movie's introduction a woman's whose hand

decorated with bangles was shaking gently across the screen. I knew immediately that this was the way I could heal our combined pain. Off I went to an Indian bangle store on University Avenue in Berkeley, California. I bought several hundred dollars worth of Indian bangles in all colors and styles.

The way they are put together is very balanced, with one main bangle in the middle and the same amount and style of bangle on each side. So if 'M' is in the middle then the combination would look like this:

B1-B2-B3-B4 - M - B4-B3-B2-B1

So one arm would have nine bangles with the main one in the middle and on each side there would be a mirror bangle to the other side. I decided to assign energetic patterns to each bangle with 'M' always being love. The center bangle represented Love, which bound both side, meaning both victim and perpetrator.

M = Love
B4 = Forgiveness
B3 = Understanding
B2 = New Beginning
B1 = Healing

When I first started out I could only wear one bangle and only for a couple of minutes. To have anything near my wrists drove me absolutely crazy. It would take several weeks to be able to wear all of them for the entire day. And every day I would put them on one at a time while praying for love, forgiveness, etc., for the victim and the perpetrator.

The first time someone said: "Wow, these are beautiful bangles," there was a streak of energy that left my wrist, it looked like a ray

of sunlight. It took me by surprise, then I saw it again. When I inquired within I realized that every time a stranger acknowledged the bangles it was not the bangles they saw and commented on, but the healing that was taking place. In complimenting the bangles they were actually anchoring the healing of yet one more victim.

It is indeed not enough to go to therapy and only heal ourselves. Especially when a crime is being committed that holds so many human souls hostage. If you have the courage to walk through your own door of fears, you will also have the means to master your fear.

Today I can wear whatever I want to around my wrists and I do not flinch or cringe when someone is grabbing me by the wrist. The fear has led to clarity, the clarity that healing can occur on a grand scale, if we only allow ourselves to be utilized for such great healing.

♥○♥

Chapter 19

Ask And You Shall Receive

♥O♥O♥O♥O♥O♥O♥O♥O♥O♥O♥O♥O♥O♥O♥O♥O♥O♥O♥O♥O♥O♥O♥O♥O♥O♥O♥O♥O♥O♥O♥

"Better indeed is knowledge than mechanical practice. Better than knowledge is meditation. But better still is surrender of attachment to results, because there follows immediate peace."

Bhagavad Gita

Ask And You Shall Receive

Before I leave you I want to impart my final story with you. You see, the world's greed has done a good job to impart on you how abundance is your birthright and that it's okay to write "I want" lists and create vision boards of your desires and longings and to do whatever it takes to get what you feel you deserve.

That's one way of living your life and personally I find that people live such lives live quite small lives. They may have the big expensive house and toys to go along with it, they may even pretend to be spiritual, but there is a sadness underlying their voice's sound waves that is unmistakable. We cannot take with us any of our worldly possessions, they only serve to distract us from what's really important here, which is the evolution of our soul. The soul hardly needs money to evolve.

Instead of lusting after materialistic possessions, what about asking for qualities of character. Gems such as discernment, courage to face and master your fears, inspiration to be about your true life's purpose, the willingness to expand your soul, kindness towards all beings at all times - things of this nature. These are the qualities that bring the conquering of fears, elimination of drama and human suffering and eradication and need for government and religious organizations.

When all humans can live by strength of character and let their simple 'yes' mean 'yes' and their 'no' mean 'no,' then we will find peace on earth.

The Day You Die

Imagine this. You just decided that it was time for your soul to move on and release your physical vessel. You stand next to your guide who is taking you to your heavenly abode. Down a long hallway you are guided with many doors on each side, each with the name of a person on it. You guide stops in front of the door with your name on it and opens the door. You look inside and as far and wide as you can see you are looking at a room filled with presents. There were wrapped gifts everyone, as far as your eyes could see. Only in the middle of the room there were a few unwrapped gifts. You turn to your guide and ask:

"Why these gifts unwrapped?"

Your guide answers: *"You see, the unwrapped gifts are the things you asked for in life, the wrapped gifts are all the things you could have gotten if you would have just asked."*

So it is my prayer that you will start asking Source for the wisdom and discernment you need to face and master your fears, to find clarity about why you are here and may you rest in peace knowing that true power and elder wisdom will follow as surely as you are following your inner guidance. You are your own inner guru!

♥O♥O♥O♥O♥O♥O♥O♥O♥O♥O♥O♥O♥O♥O♥O♥O♥O♥O♥O♥O♥O♥O♥O♥O♥O♥O♥O♥O♥O♥O♥O♥

Chapter 20

Time Line

♥♡♥

"He who falls in love with himself will have no rivals."

Benjamin Franklin

Time Line

The following is a time line, both for the past and future visions, which are explained in more detail throughout the book. The numbers after the title reflect my age at that time.

1971: First Near Death Experience (5)

Took a bad fall, died. Concussion, stitches. Regained consciousness knowing that this life was a dream, the 'other side' was real. Appearance of 'the voice,' funnels, vortexes, energies and other geometric symbols in the 'sky.' Withdrawal from humans, society. Was asked not to speak about it.

1971: Spiritual Experience (5)

Periphery twirled and appearance of farm ahead caused revelation of purpose of masculine and feminine. Felt enveloped by Source energy.

1973: Felt Called To Vegetarianism (7)

Easter Sunday; parents served rabbit for dinner; I was convinced we were single handedly responsible for ending Easter for all of humanity. Given vision of myself at 50 years of age.

1978: Lost Interest in Life (12)

Family split apart, lost interest in life, started research on most effective method to commit suicide.

1981: Second Near Death Experience (15)

Travel through the tunnel, realizing sound creates and destroys everything; was told to find the "keys to instant manifestations;" hand dissolving into light, transparent cube of information downloaded into my 'system.' Visions continued; became utterly fascinated with esoteric subjects, learned dowsing, I-Ching, meditation, etc. Moved out into a horseback riding stable to spend three years in solitude. Started feeling dead people; was scared of the feeling.

1984: Decided to Live (18)

Decided to live fully in this physical body, got engaged, completed a degree, learned another language, went to work for a private bank in Switzerland. Visions continued pouring in; no one to talk to.

1989: Moved to the United States (23)

Arrived in San Francisco with two suitcases, $500 in my pocket and speaking no English. Learned English while watching Oprah.

1991: Third Near Death Experience (25)

Overdosed on anesthesia from three emergency surgeries immediately before wedding. Visited someone else's 'heaven' and was asked to bring message back to a living person. Got married. Visions rapidly expanded. Made contact with my first personal guide, his name was Seth. Not 'the' Seth, a new baby angel, I was his first student, he was my first guide. Answers were limited to 'yes,' 'no,' maybe,' 'sometimes,' etc. New guides continued appearing until I had learned what I needed to learn from them.

1993: Birth of our Daughter (27)

The birth and spiritual unfolding of our daughter catapulted my own spiritual development to new heights. Started to see dead people and spirits.

1996: Lymphoma (30)

Was sent home by the Infectious Disease Specialist with six weeks to six months live. Asked to put my affairs in order and create last Will and testament. Daughter was 2.5 years old. Voice returned - spiritual revelation. New guides appeared, a King and Queen joined as one, like Siamese twins. She is wearing the masculine, red/orange/yellow colors and he is wearing the feminine colors, green/blue/purple. Solomon also appeared. Calls himself Shulamin or Solamun. Not sure of spelling, hearing is not my most defined skills. He doesn't mind.

2000: Spiritual Unfolding Continues (34)

Developed mind reading skills; continued seeing more beings, including non-earthly beings, aliens, angels. Asked to see everything (do not ask for this unless you are prepared to meet the dark side, I'm not kidding). Asked for wisdom to be able to handle what I would see, and wisdom to be guided on what my work is here. Other, much more advanced guides appear.

2004: Separation from Husband (38)

The shedding of a non-beneficial marriage propelled me forward extensively in my spiritual work. Visions continued pouring in. Work on the 'other side' revealed itself to clearing souls stuck in rifts throughout the planet (from tragic earth events, natural disasters, mega accidents and other mass deaths); collecting rainbows from the 'field of rainbow;' am known as the 'rainbow weaver' and 'rainbow collector' on the other side. Am not a light worker, am a balance worker.

2005: Lemurians

Guided to reconnect with Lemuria. Regularly communicating with them. New guides showing up in the field of science, astrology, relationships. Solomon and the Siamese King and Queen continue to be major guides too.

2006: Giving Over Life

Asked God to take over the stirring wheel and fully dedicated my life to live the second part as the passenger. "Show me what you

got," I said. Do not pray this unless you are prepared to have your "I" dismantled and rebuilt in the hot furnace where diamonds get refinished again and again.

Was given the task to become celibate, to stop eating, stop associating with groups and not be a part of society and to stop reading books. My job was to find my inner guru. Was groomed for healing work; able to get others' headache away in 30-90 seconds; started seeing inside people's bodies by only hearing their names and age (without having to meet them). Started to see energy strands and being able to 'follow them' to find the original 'cause' of something. Also got a date of January 18, 2052, but don't know why.

2007: Dying Again

Almost died of a ruptured appendix. Got sicker and sicker, started to eat less and less, sometimes not at all. Knew I would have to put conscious effort into stop eating all together but still didn't know why. Diet switched to prepare for the journey.

2008: Looking For Aneurism

Woke up with face and eye drooping. Was told I either had a stroke, aneurism or a tumor. Diagnosed with several immune deficiencies. Four years later eye is still 'broken' but doctors haven't found anything.

2008-2009: 'Get Out'

Kept hearing 'get out' of California but did not receive visions or answers of why. Messages kept coming closer and closer together and becoming more urgent. In 2009 I felt my energy pull back completely, did not even want to go outside but was definitely not depressed. A move was inevitable, I felt no longer 'at home' in California. Contemplated moving to New Zealand, Canada, India or France; researched all places.

2010: Moving to Italy

Was eventually guided to move to the Italian alps in the north. Solitude and silence was key. Was sure I would never return to the U.S., sold or gave away everything, had no more ties to the U.S.. Finding my inner guru in nature was paramount.

2011: Moving to Switzerland

Was guided to move to the Swiss alps and instructed not to lock myself down in form of lease, furniture, etc. Got a used scooter instead of a car. Learned from big lizard looking like 'spirit' of the plan the dark side has for humanity. He looked like a T-rex dinosaur, communication was telepathic. He showed me how they are located in churches throughout the world depositing little specks of their 'data' in the energetic field of the unassuming humans. He explained that churches have lost their energetic powers and that they have been 'hanging out' in churches for a long time because people would come with open, hopeful and gullible hearts, which he explained, was the perfect energetic consistency for them to implant their speck of data. The energy fields of humans are down. Then he showed me the

people leave to go back to their homes, their countries, taking these specks with them, where they serve as "cell towers" for the reptilians. Moving above the earth's field looking down I saw what the entire structure looked like. If you can imagine a spider's web that has been destroyed, then the spider rebuilds it but it won't be as good as the first time, then it gets destroyed again, the spider rebuilds it. Eventually the web looks ugly and distorted. This is what he showed me, they are building on the surface of the planet. Their net is about 1-2 feet above in the realm where most mental and intellectual energy spends their time. Where there are no humans the net touches to the ground. Their net serves as a controlling device and mental programming device.

I pulled myself up above the world's grid and saw another weave outside of the earth's energy grid, this weave was rainbow colored and perfect. It is the weave that is being spun and held together by the 'light' side.

I had entered the church with a friend of mine and the T-rex was getting ready to deposit his speck of data into my friends shield; I projected my energy field to protect him and the T-rex was not successful in depositing into him, it took all of my strength and when we left the church we both were very nauseated and had intense stomach aches. My friend didn't know what happened but felt the evil presence.

I asked the Being why he wasn't depositing into me and he said: "we're not allowed to touch you." I asked him why but he didn't know. It wasn't until a few months later that I saw a golden shield around me with countless controls inside. I literally look like I'm in my own spaceship, which is just the size of a bubble around me. I have no idea what these controls are all for and don't touch them, somehow they do their own thing.

After seeing that I could extend my shield over my friend who was maybe 10 yards away, I attempted to shield others half way across the planet. While it can be done, little golden Beings appeared who are doing some sort of 'sowing' job to sever a piece of my shield and create a new shield I am protecting, they 'sow' the shields so they become indestructible. I do not ever extend the shield unless I am asked for it. I am clearly guided not to do things for people unless they ask. It's called free will and it must be honored always

February 2012: Moving Back to the U.S.

Heard loud and clear that I would need to move back to the United States. When I asked 'why' I heard *"rebuild"* over and over again. I did not get any specific visions as to what or whom I was to help rebuild. Was asked to stay away from coasts.

May 2012: Moved to Sedona, Arizona

Guidance to fully integrate living on no food.

August 2012: Last Meal

Spirit became more and more urgent to live on no food and heard that eventually I would not need water. Went for only one hike and barely made it. Visions started to pour in. Rubble and devastation everywhere, looked like an earthquake but there was also a lot of ash. People dying or dead already. Saw myself skinny but healthy, going from person to person to see who was still alive. People in white hazmat suits appeared, they were spraying

something. When they saw me they asked how it was possible I was alive. I said *"I don't know."* These visions were recurring.

September 2012: Barefoot Hiking

First four weeks of not eating were the hardest, hunger feeling intense in week two and week four. Spirit now urged me to hike the red rocks of Arizona barefoot and to spend several hours a day in nature and in the sun. Started sun gazing, max one minute a day. Was guided to hike 1 hour a day, on no food, and to reduce water to one ounce per day. Hunger feelings completely gone, weight loss too excessive; asked body to start gaining size; went from size 0 to size 4 in two weeks. A whole new level of commanding my own body, love it. Started to hear vegetables and fruits talk to me. Have been hearing animals including bugs but hearing fruit having consciousness is quite something.

October 2012: No Water

Was asked to reduce water intake to three sips per day and increase hiking to 3 hours per day, barefoot. Facing huge fears, dying of thirst. Day 1 without water, awesome; day 3 without water, feeling like I'm hovering over the rocks instead of touching them; day 4 without water, realizing that my body's balancing system is completely off; everything is lighter, I am floating; felt often like my feet didn't touch the ground. Happiness increased hugely to a state of true bliss. Day 8 of no water, feeling the shedding of ego and all beliefs, blissful state cannot be described. Body feeling beautiful and full of energy. Meditated on Cathedral Rock hearing conscious souls 'stuck' inside the mountain, asking for mercy, expressing readiness to move up the evolutionary ladder once again. Seeing lives of stuck souls having fallen by

their graces. Hearing Spirit clearly and seeing visions of what is hell and what is heaven. Overwhelmed at the visions.

December 21, 2012:

Spent the transition time with my Soul and in love. Getting many visions of symbols being downloaded, visible in periphery; vortexes and funnels are displaying a huge 'light show.' Major shifts taking place; world completely unaware.

2013:

Seeing water damage everywhere. Water appearing where there wasn't any before. Clear visions of largest area of physical earth changes coming from underneath New Zealand and South America. Seeing the Pacific ocean bed as clear as the back of my hand. Ocean underneath ocean. Two ocean beds. Second ocean beneath is completely toxic, cannot crack or air will become toxic waste. Volcano underneath New Zealand's second ocean so big it makes Yellow Stone look like a pebble. Not seeing 'THE' big earthquake for 2013 but many that are big enough and close enough to each other that the 'big' volcano under New Zealand will cause some cracks and instigate other earthquakes. Won't erupt above sea level but be big enough to cause New Zealand to restructure itself and cause damage in South America and Australia. Not sure about North New Zealand, doesn't feel good. Earthquakes there cause ripple effects of other earthquakes up the coast all the way to Alaska. Seeing number 8.2, 8.7, 9.4, 12 and 13, but don't know where. Feeling that 12 and 13 are underneath the ocean, and will cause the shifting of much of the landscape.

When tuning into extra terrestrials and 'dark energies' I see the South pole, New Zealand area to be their hub. Much energy for them is drawn from this massive volcano. The North pole has been a hub for many other extra terrestrials. Seeing a gateway in both areas. New Zealand's gateway is 'closed' to the human eye. North pole area (somewhere off Norway, etc.), is open to the human eye but when I ask why we are not aware of it I am being told by their guardians that mind control is at play. Humans have indeed tried to find the 'place' and have been right on top of it but they are being prevented from actually seeing the gateway, even though it is right in front of their eyes. The Beings are tall, at least 8-10 feet, dark, dark green with scaly skin that is shimmering with gold. When they talk, even though it's telepathic, I feel drunk. They do not use 'regular language' or voices; their advanced state of civilization is using a much different sound wave technique to communicate. It sounds more like music. They wear some kind of armor but it's not for protection. I do not see males and females, they all feel unisex to me. They are kind and they are not to be feared.

They explain that the gateway there has been an access channel for many extra terrestrials, not just them. Most of them get along, with the exception of those that gather in the South pole area.

From what they are telling me the ones to be cautious of, once they reveal themselves to humanity, are the grays and certain types of greens. There are two types of greens from the Pleiadians; one very kind, the other very evil. And then there is another type of green, not from the Pleiadians, not sure where they're from but they cannot be trusted. When I ask how to know the difference they said they can be recognized by their facial features just like humans who can't be trusted. Others have no facial expression, it's like they are dead, but they do

communicate telepathically. You will know, follow internal guidance.

There are many others that appeared; golden ones, little ones and tall golden ones. Very light blue, almost fluorescent blue ones, white ones. All kind and here to help although they may not reveal themselves to humans. We see them with the inner eyes.

When I asked about reptilians and the grey ones I am being told that they've been roaming earth for millions of years. They are without soul and are an artificial intelligence with the soul purpose of soul harvesting. Souls that are attempted to be lured in by them may make a contract with them; they may be threatened of going to hell or else make an agreement with them to live out another human life based on their terms.

Visions of galactic ships assembling in our Universe has become overwhelming. If you have ever seen the San Francisco Bay during the Blue Angel flight days, then you know how packed the bay is with sailboats and yachts on those days. That is what the Universe looks like right now; mother ships of all kinds. Some to help, some to watch and learn, some to harvest and destroy, some to clean up.

When I ask what humanity can do I always get the same message: realize you are Source. Humans with souls are therefore higher than the angels. Angels are here to assist us. Instant liberation can be achieved. What must be done is TVs and radios be turned off, no magazines and newspapers be red. These are the tools used for mass entrainment, to mass brain wash humans into wasting time with unimportant things. Humans now are worried about diet, GMO labeling, white collar criminals and terrorist attacks. All of these things are only used to stir people away from themselves and their own magnificence.

I am being told that these things will continue to happen in greater numbers, more devastating and closer together. It's as if a copper wire that was in a straight line is now being wrapped up in a coil. With every turn the energy running through it gains speed. These events are causing massive energies that will eventually cause something to pop. That popping needs to be humanity waking up NOW. Peace must first be found within before it can be found without.

2013 - 2017:

Asked to move to Los Angeles. What in the world!? Suddenly being given visions that my own death would be near, urged to get my affairs together and write this book was of utmost importance.

April 2013: Was guided to eat very little but no live foods, only nuts and seeds. I have learned that it is entire possible to live without food but the journey to get there is only for those that are called by Spirit, otherwise it is starvation. So please do not undertake this journey! My job was to know that I could live without food and that perhaps one day I would have to teach and encourage people the switch over when it gets to a place where we really don't have any edible foods. When I inquire about the future of our food and water supply I keep seeing disturbing visions of massive food and water poisoning and shortages. Some of it man induced, some of it environmentally induced. It's not about storing food, it's about learning how to live on very little.

Continued earth changes. Saw population reduction of at least a quarter if not more than half through various methods. Seeing explosions, implosions; all of the planet will change. It's not about finding a safe place, it's about finding your inner guru, trusting

your guidance and knowing that you are always divinely guided and protected. The work now is internal, not external. Keep hearing "let go" over and over again.

Also seeing some kind of chemical substance cover the planet, close to the ground, in the ground or on the ground, but it originated somewhere else, air or above the planet, not sure. Feels like it is man made most likely. Causes some kind of suffocation for the planet, not the people, and is the cause for some strange weather changes. Weather changes look natural but are not at all.

Seeing the Northern lights coming towards the equator in the Middle East in the middle of the day. Seeing soldiers and others look up in awe, dropping their weapons and wanting to come home. Instant change on a heart level. This is a major signal for the earth changes to start happening, although I see them happening over the next 2-3 years. Everything will change, much will be lost.

Full integration of the seven-nervous center must take place; we are being upgraded to a nine-nervous center, which must be complete by 2027. Those who are not integrating now will refold and start anew. I see a seal on people's forehead, it's in their third eye and looks like a shining bright light - people without the seal will not make it. I asked about the seal and was shown a golden liquid, oily substance, which is flowing from the first chakra up the spine and into the glands in the head, especially the pineal gland. Humanity is self destructing the rising of this oil through alcohol, drugs, non-sacred sexual activities and other sense oriented behaviors. Eating meat and excessive dairy also changes its chemical make-up. Purity is of the utmost importance now.

I see a combination of several things that will cause the changes. Major solar flares, possible meteorites (daughter sees *"fire falling from the sky and rubble and ash everywhere"*). Note that she also sees our police force, army and other armed guards to become those to fear. There are 2-3 deadly viruses being unleashed by the governments. One I hear is from Mars and has no antidote. I am told the government is holding this virus and they know it can cause total world human eradication. If this virus gets out humanity will be over. I don't see this one getting out but it's there for future destructive uses. The other one or two we will create an antidote for but not in time to save most.

Anti-Christ is being prepared for appearance in 2022 or 2023. He is currently a banker and very philanthropic. Doesn't know he's being used by the dark side.

There are many so-called light workers now that are completely unaware that they are being used by the dark side. The dark side is creating portals through these light-workers, to be activated during some of these occurrences.

THE WORLD DOES NOT NEED LIGHT WORKERS. THE WOLD DESPERATELY NEEDS BALANCE WORKERS.

Every light worker must be matched by its counter part to keep the equilibrium of the Universe. Every light worker literally creates another dark worker. The dark side knows this, so the more light workers that can be created, the more dark workers on their side will be created as well. We desperately need balance workers who hold the infinity symbol in place from its center.

May 2013: Waking up with two dreams back to back about enormous breaker waves several hundred meters tall creating

massive destruction. I can't tell where I am, it doesn't look familiar, all I see is being surrounded by water everywhere.

Second dream was in same location but massive, black cloud overhead formed to create a tornado filled with water, sunlight and black clouds. The sunlight made the enormous tornado glisten from within. There was a sense that the black cloud formation was man made but that the sunlight contained within the tornado was trying to counter act the direction or damage of the tornado.

After inquiring with Spirit I kept hearing 'baptism through fire' again and again. I saw fire falling from the skies and explosions taking place. I didn't see forest fires started by arsonists, these fires were related to things exploding or things falling. I kept hearing again and again 'baptism through fire' when suddenly flashes of visions of the flood in Noah's times were flashing before me. I had the clear sense that 'back then' the earth needed to be baptized through water, which was evident from the time of Noah all the way through the time of Jesus up until today. The Piscean age symbolized baptism through water.

We have entered the Aquarian age, Aquarius being an air sign. I got the strong sense that because of 'air' these fires are explosive. This includes volcanoes, man made explosions, meteorites, sun flares.

When I ask for the number of humanity being refined by fire I get no clear numbers but in the first dream only five of approximately thirty of us survived.

It has become more and more evident by the day that refinement by fire is a necessity for everyone wanting to ascend. There is no free ride. We either walk our journey and work consciously and

willingly with Spirit to grow and learn or off in the heavenly oven shall we go for more lessons and more refinement.

Remember, eternity is a long time, that's how long we get to do this again and again.

2017 - 2022:

I see life change. This is a period where I get very different visions. It's almost like it hasn't been decided yet which reality will come to pass, as if "this is humanity's choice." I see 'evil people' wanting to force the one world order, which would be eventual death for humanity. And I also see the population becoming a lot more peaceful, in those visions I don't see the one-world order come to pass.

2022-2023:

I find myself in a station or library, huddled with hundreds of others who have come for shelter. The windows look fire red, with either real fire outside or the sun being extremely hot. There is no food and no water. The Anti-Christ steps in, tall man, wearing a robe. He promises to save people if they go with him. He introduces himself as Jesus but his initials are SK. He explains that just like people and times change, he too needed to take on a new name. People will fall for it. I stand up and exclaim that he is the Anti-Christ and not to follow him, to listen to their inner guru so they could see the darkness in him. Only 4 people stay with me, hundreds go with him straight to their deaths.

You will recognize him by the "good deeds" he is doing now. He will be the "former banker who has turned guru" and will have

won many hearts over the next few years as a philanthropist, so that when the time comes people trust him based on his actions. It's a set up.

2023-2027:

I don't get much for this period, things are still up in the air and contingent on what humanity decides as a whole. Seeing my daughter with a little boy and a little girl.

2027-2029:

Integration from the 7-nervous center to the 9-nervous center is to be completed. If this completes, which it will for those who are still here, there will be an entire new way of walking and caring for the planet. I see peace everywhere. Simple life but with the added on benefits of technology. Earning a living will have changed methods although I'm not sure if the use of money has completely disappeared. I still see currency of some sort being exchanged.

2029-2052:

I don't get much for this time and am told that it is just like the period from 2023-2029 and will depend on what people decide. I do the option for peace after 2017, but it will all depend on the population waking up.

I see January 18, 2052 an important date for myself. I will be 85 then and it could be that this is my refolding day. Then again, I have felt my physical parting to be very close. When I ask Spirit I

am told that I need to learn how to do my etheric work in a more refined way while I am in the body so that when so many souls are shedding their temples I can help them move on rather than get stuck and exposed to the 'bardo snatchers.' The number of souls that will be stuck in rifts on the planet will cause the remaining humans barely able to recover from the agony of their capture. It is imperative that we learn how to free our souls NOW so that when the time of our shedding happens we know exactly what to do.

At this time I have learned that the message "rebuild" was for this world while also helping on the 'other side' with the souls that will be stuck on this place.

I see my daughter still alive by the time I am 85; I live alone and die alone.

♥O♥O♥O♥O♥O♥O♥O♥O♥O♥O♥O♥O♥O♥O♥O♥O♥O♥O♥O♥O♥O♥O♥O♥O♥O♥O♥O♥O♥O♥O♥

There are several more visions that are unimportant at this time and they are being refined. Dear reader, please take this with a huge bolder of salt! This is neither meant to scare you nor is this the holy grail. On the contrary. We are talking about Spirit, energy, as etheric and 'fluid' as energy can get, everything can change. Everything is hopefully changing already, for the better. It must start with you. Instead of buy up a bunch of food and water, which would only be an act of desperation, and therefore not the most beneficial energy, use the mantras in this book and read the rest of this book with your heart.

This is a book for your soul. This is a book, a tiny nugget, to help you in your unfolding process. And the unfolding and ascension process is all about remembering the magnificence of who you

are. You are Source. Indestructible, all-knowing, all-permeating, you are eternity!

♥0♥0♥0♥0♥0♥0♥0♥0♥0♥0♥0♥0♥0♥0♥0♥0♥0♥0♥0♥0♥0♥0♥0♥0♥0♥0♥0♥0♥0♥0♥

Chapter 21

What You Can Do

♥0♥0♥0♥0♥0♥0♥0♥0♥0♥0♥0♥0♥0♥0♥0♥0♥0♥0♥0♥0♥0♥0♥0♥0♥0♥0♥0♥0♥0♥0♥0♥

"Love is like unto the ascent of a mountain. It comes ever nearer to you as you go ever nearer to it."

Lao Russell

What You Can Do

While I hope you are still reading my story, what I really hope for is to have sparked a divine little flicker inside your soul so that you remember your true magnificence. Every time you say *"I am"* you are declaring that you are God. And you are. But do you really know this with all of your might? Is there still any doubt in you about the power and magnificence that is awaiting you?

If there is, I would like to encourage you, no, I would like to urge you now to get your act together and wake up. This is not a dress rehearsal, this is not practice, this is your life and at best only a flicker of an eye in the bigger picture of eternity. The alarm clock has gone off, the time is now.

The time is running out for many in the flesh and whether you are on 'this side' with a physical temple or you decide to move on some place else without a physical vessel, you need to know that **the power of your choices permeate all space and surpass linear time.**

Let me repeat this so that when you get 'there' you will remember.

THE POWER OF CHOICE PERMEATES ALL SPACE AND SURPASSES LINEAR TIME.

In other words, even when your physical body's life has come to an end and you find yourself standing over your body, the greatest power you will have in that moment is choice. Remember this always!

Let me give you an example.

Your Future Higher Self

I was asked to check into someone's health when he gave me permission to call in his guides or his higher self for assistance. Immediately a Being appeared that later presented himself as the person's 'Future Higher Self.' Just like with the ghost who split himself into four I didn't know that our future higher selves could actually travel back through linear time to give us warnings and messages. I asked him to show me how he did this and he showed me a rainbow colored worm hole that shot through time and space the way we know it. He was here out of desperation to save this person's soul. The person was not on the right track and the choices he was making would result in an early and unnecessary refolding.

You can do the same. You can call in your own higher self, your guides, and you can ask for guidance. Remember that you must ask in order for you to receive. And you must ask with all of your mind and all of your soul and all of your heart. Otherwise it's just a question that may go unanswered.

Getting Your Life Together

People often think that 'getting their life together' means to have your last Will documented, your assets divided and your funeral prearranged. And while it is very considerate of you to take care of such details as these unresolved issues can cause serious family divisions down the line, what is really more important for your soul is to be ready. So let me ask you this:

Is your soul ready?

This is the real question. Has your soul had a chance to experience its magnificence through your vessel? Do you even know what the soul is? Have you given your magnificent self enough life and love to experience true expansion?

If you haven't and you are still wasting time chasing after a career, after money, after girls or guys or the relationship that will surely be a band aid to your aching heart, it is now time to wake up. I cannot stress this enough.

Do not worry about whether or not your vessel is going to make it, this is not about physical survival. Your body is temporary, your soul, however, lives on forever. Your soul is eternal. Do you have any idea where you are going?

If not, this is the time to really make peace and reunite with your soul, ask your higher self questions, lots of them. Ask your Spirit guides to guide you.

Changing Your Story

For a long time my mantra sounded like this:

"My parents didn't want me, I was hit and punished needlessly, I was kicked out of my home when I was fifteen and I never heard 'I love you' growing up. All I heard was that I would never amount to anything, that I was a loser and that I was a quitter."

I had heard these things all my life growing up and understandably they became corner stones for me to live my life by. Everything in my life had to reflect these beliefs that I had adopted to be my truth. And life gladly supported me until one day I realized that I could change the story of my life.

Today my story sounds very different, it sounds more like this:

"I had the best childhood ever, growing up next to a farm I learned everything there was to learn about couples working as a team for the greater benefit of the village that counted on them. I learned how to make everything from scratch, I churned butter, baked bread from and made jam from scratch, I ate corn on the cob raw right there in the field. And when I finally asked my parents questions about their own upbringing I started to understand that the way they parented me was done with so much love compared to their own upbringing, and a flood of compassion and unconditional love for them mixed with deep gratitude for having given me a roof over my head and not sending me away the way their parents did. I am truly blessed to have been asked to earn my own money at such an early age, it built my character and it gave me the sense of independence, all of which is serving me so well today."

My sister and I on the farm, me on the tractor

You see, I can look at my parents and blame them but last time I checked blame has never healed any wounds of the heart as of yet.

The backpack filled with pain, distain, hatred and judgment was on my back and I was schlepping this thing through my life and I was tired of the burden.

Have I ever been able to get resolution from my parents?

No. I have tried, again and again, until I realized that I was just looking to be heard and understood.

I wanted them to apologize and see how much they hurt me. But that's not how forgiveness works. Forgiveness is based on no conditions or ultimatums.

Today I have not only mended my relationship with my parents but I love them dearly. I always remember that they did the very best they could with what they were given. Today they are still the same people and frankly I marvel at how I have chosen to be born to people like my parents. The mismatch is mind boggling and at the same time it is because of this energetic mismatch that I am who I am today. And there is not one split second of my life that I would want to trade. I have found that the fountain of unconditional love and compassion within me has brought the healing that we all needed and an apology is not needed, not from anyone, because the peace, love, understanding and forgiveness sprung froth from within me.

Forgiveness

People often ask me if I had ever forgiven my mom and my dad and my answer is always the same: "of course!" All of the following emotions are toddler emotions. And by that I mean they are immature, unevolved emotions, which have no benefit but to assist you in throwing a temper tantrum just like any three year old:

- Anger
- Grudges
- Bitterness
- Jealousy

- Lack of Forgiveness
- Hatred
- Revenge
- Depression
- Manipulation
- Craftiness
- etc.

What a waste of time and insult to your soul's true magnificence!

I have tried several times to talk to my mother about the incident and the hitting but there is no getting anywhere with my mother. She is just not evolved enough and that is okay. If a person doesn't get it, that's okay. It's not them that need to get it. You do because you are holding the lack of forgiveness and carry the bitterness that is eating away at you, not them. It is not mine to avenge myself, that is not my job. My job is to be love and then extend that to those around me. No exception.

You may feel like there is no one whom you haven't forgiven yet and feel pretty good with yourself. Good for you. Here is a test question for you.

If Hitler were to come into your room and asked to sit with you and ask for forgiveness, could you get up, hug him and truly forgive him?

Now be honest about how you just felt at just my mentioning his name. If there is any discomfort you have not yet forgiven. Keep going.

Facing And Mastering Fear

My Mayan Astrologist told me that all of humanity must pass through four doors:

Door 1: Fear
Door 2: Clarity
Door 3: Power
Door 4: Wisdom

Everyone wants clarity!

"What is my purpose here?"
"What is life all about?"
"Where is the love of my life?"

And yet the reason we are not getting answers is because we refuse to go through the door of fear, which must be mastered before the door of clarity becomes even visible to us.

Once we are through the door of clarity we enter into the powerful phases of life. Having mastered fears and having lived a life of clarity will give us unshakeable power, which eventually will lead us to elder wisdom.

Everyone wants clarity and everyone wants power. We see this often in famous, powerful adults who in reality are just scared little boys and girls lusting for a false kind of power. Not having gone through their door of fears they may appear to be powerful but their power is neither long lasting nor will it lead to elder wisdom. On the contrary, their fall is imminent.

Don't be that way!

It is not enough to just face your fears, you must master them. Facing them and fighting them will be like a dragon whose head you cut off and suddenly he grows three more heads. And no, the answer is not to kill the dragon either. Rather learn how to tame the dragon and then use him as your pet. If you do this right he will fly you to new heights you never even imagined possible.

Love overcomes all. No exception. It's pretty simple. Whatever you fear you are in the process of becoming. Let me say this again.

WHATEVER YOU FEAR YOU ARE IN THE PROCESS OF BECOMING.

If you truly want to master you fear you will make it your mission to love it, unconditionally. For me this was public speaking. More than ten years ago I would have rather died than share in a group. Remember, I was the little girl who was introduced as the shy one. Today public speaking is my biggest passion. Not because I'm that great at it but because my soul was giving me the opportunity to turn my biggest fear into my biggest joy. And as this tilting occurred my soul was able to evolve. That is what this whole life is all about. Find your soul's own stirrings and messages, it is calling out to you and wanting desperately live its life fully through you.

Ask your soul what it wants. Then listen.

Powerful Mantras

Here are a couple of powerful mantras for you to memorize and recite every day throughout your day. Replace your mind's chatter with these beautiful mantras and watch peace come over you. Do not under estimate the power of these mantras. They

have saved me many times from being in the wrong place at the wrong time. This will become even more important in just the near future.

"I choose to know nothing and allow the divine spark of my soul to lay before me all things possible."

"I am divinely guided and protected and always in the right place at the right time."

Here is what one of our community member had to say about the second mantra:

> *"It is a mantra that has really brought me a new heavenly peace I have never felt before. I see purpose in everything, everywhere. It brings me a happiness and joy that bring me to tears, it brought me back to the awareness of the Divinity that envelops me in every moment."* **Ava**

Do not underestimate these mantras, they may just kick off the lid that is so tightly screwed to your Pandora's box. It's time to set yourself free.

Meditation and Nature

Many people tell me that they just can't meditate, it's just too hard for them, they can't sit still or whatever their excuse is. I'm a quadruple Gemini with a moon in Aquarius, basically this means that I think for a dozen people all at the same time. I have rarely met a person who can multi-task as fast and as well as me. Thinking, typing, communicating, learning, expanding are musts for me, and I do it at high speed. With plenty of Mars and Pluto in

my chart to make sure that not only sitting still would be difficult for me but nearly impossible, you can imagine that learning how to sit still and quiet my mind was nearly impossible.

I could have used all of these things as excuses and I often did when I gave up on meditation, it was just too frustrating. Who had time to sit still or while getting frustrated with the gazillion thoughts that would keep rushing in when all I wanted to do was shut off my thinking? It nearly drove me nuts. I really get it.

And yet, this is exactly what I mean by not only facing your fear but actually mastering them. There is nothing that would have been simpler than to not learn how to go within into silence. It would have been the easy route. But remember that Albert Einstein said that *"the one who walks alone, is likely to find himself in places no one has ever been."* There is no place as sacred and holy as the place of your inner sanctuary. And only you can get yourself there.

Whether you want to learn how to expand your intuition, get in touch with your soul or simply experience more peace or better health, meditation is a must-include practice in your daily routine.

No more excuses!

The Power of Water

It is said that Earth consists of approximately 90% water and ideally our bodies too ideally consist of this much water; although diet and age have a lot to do with this percentage to be much lower in our physical vessel.

Water is the easiest, simplest and most magical elixir to send love and healing from you to the world.

Dr. Emoto Masuru has shown in his photographs that water programmed with certain words or music crystallize into specific shapes of snow flakes. We know that words such as 'I love you' or 'I hate you' will create completely different water crystals.

Self talk, whether beneficial or non-beneficial, affects not only us but the entire planet. 'How so,' you may ask? Because we all have an excretory system and the water content of our bodies will leave our bodies to become one again with our water filtration system and eventually the ground, travel back to the creeks and rivers of the world to be united once again with our big oceans.

Your words, your thoughts and your actions hold more power than anything else on this planet. If you want to truly have an impact on this world, for the better, than you must start to become more aware of your own thoughts and your own patterns and habits of speech.

To take this a step further, use water to create deliberate intentions. Here are just a few examples:

- Write little love notes to yourself and for the world on sticky notes and place them underneath your water.

- When you pray, do so holding your finger or hand in a cup of water; when finished with your prayer release the water (prayer) down the drain to infiltrate the water of the entire planet.

- Do the same when you walk out in nature, either pray holding your hands or feet in a creek or the ocean or pray

with your hand in the water at home and take the water bottle with you out into nature where you release the water.

This does not just apply to water, you can put love notes inside your refrigerator to recalibrate all of your refrigerator's contents.

Let your guidance system unfold the endless possibilities here! What's important is that you start being crucially aware of your thoughts, your speech and your actions. Wake up and as you do, you will start to touch things with a reverence for life that you may never have experienced before. Including the miracle of water.

Get Support and Become Your Own Guru

While my biggest message is for you to learn to think for yourself and to make your own choices, you must also find your own guru within. We are, as a collective humanity, in a place now, where we have to find our own master within. There is absolutely nothing and no one 'out there' able or capable of teaching you anything that you do not already know on a soul level. Every so-called teacher out there is only here to regurgitate something that only stirs your memory. Your job is to remember.

Run from people, especially spiritual people who tell you that you must have a master to follow and that you must be initiated by this or that in order to get salvation. What tragedy to be told such nonsense. YOU initiate yourself by raising your own vibration, and you do this by waking up, by getting out of the matrix, by being willing to get your heart drive swept clean. You must be willing to do the work. There is no free ride and if anyone ever tells you that

participating in their program will help your ascension or raise you to the 5th dimension - run!

There are no more predators, knowingly or unknowingly, than in the field of spirituality. Rightfully so since we know government is not our leader and can't be trusted. Neither can world religions be trusted, especially not with your soul's health and well being. Business doesn't give a darn about your soul, they're only interested in money. This leaves every person who calls themselves a spiritual teacher, guide or guru. Above all you must learn that you must first be your own guru. You must learn to trust your own intuition. When you learn this, others who are finding their own guru within are joining on your path and together you will share your experiences as a collective family.

Self Care

So many of us know that we need to first fill our own cup to the brim so we can then overflow and be giving to those around us. And yet reality is often very different than this. We take care of everyone around us, our spouses, children, bosses and then, if there is any time left over we take a little tiny bit of a sliver of time for ourselves and the worst part is, we even feel guilty about it. This has to stop.

You must learn to practice self care.

It's quite simple. Make a list with three columns. Here is what you'll write in each column:

Column 1: Write down all the things you love doing (taking a bubble bath, baking, going out with friends, writing an uplifting card for a friend, etc.)

Column 2: Write down things you don't like doing but make you feel better once they're done (ironing, cleaning, working out, grocery shopping, etc.)

Column 3: Write down things you dislike doing and they don't make you feel better even after you do them (paying bills perhaps?)

Each day you'll pick three things from column 1 and three things from column 2 and just go do them. Important: For column 3 you'll just have to hire someone or you'll drive yourself crazy. It's not worth it getting negative energy into your daily life more than is necessary.

If this system doesn't appeal to you, that's fine, just do something that creates a system of accountability for your own self care. It's actually a little sad that we have to create systems to assure our own self care, but this is the life we have created for ourselves. It's now time to re-arrange our priorities.

Finding Freedom At Your Core

From my childhood to approaching my fifties, having lived without the attachments of what I clung to for dear life for so long, I am here to tell you that true freedom at your core can only be found by you and within you. Everyone is a teacher. I created a video about one of my greatest lessons learned from a cockroach. I have learned important lessons from ants, a banana, puppies, flowers, trees, children, adults and most of all from within the sacred silence that can only be found within the depth of your core.

Many years ago I decided to create a place people can call a *'home away from home.'* A community where people can come and feel at home, where men and women can share their journeys with other like-minded people. There is no one leader better than anyone else; everyone is a teacher. We believe that when you came into this world you brought a light with you that wasn't there before. It is your life's mission to now spread this light into the world. What are your spreading? Therefore we want you to come shine your light in our community. That's how important our members are.

We discuss topics related to the evolution of your soul. A personal life skills community that has helped many members find new courage and above all, has helped them connect with their own inner guru.

You can find us in the resources section or go directly to www.CoreFreedom.com.

Chapter 22

Summary

♥0♥0♥0♥0♥0♥0♥0♥0♥0♥0♥0♥0♥0♥0♥0♥0♥0♥0♥0♥0♥0♥0♥0♥0♥0♥0♥0♥0♥0♥

"All problems and unhappy conditions of humans are due to a breach somewhere of the law of balance. "

Walter Russell

Summary

I said I would write this book in two days and the second day is now coming to an end. I could go on and on but what needed to be said is said and those who have ears, have heard. Those of you have eyes, see with your own eyes.

We do not have much time and the unfolding of your soul is of utmost importance. I dare say that nothing in this Universe is as important as your soul. Your soul is all-wise, all-knowing, it knows the way. It is our human life that is wanting to find balance and integrate soul with our beautiful, magnificent human vessels. Listen.

Remember Lao Tzu's words: *"At the center of your being you have the answer. You know who you are and you know what you want."*

Instead of chasing after the next romantic partner, new car or next million dollars, take Ram Dass' advice to heart: *"I would like my life to be a statement of love and compassion - and where it isn't that's where my work lies."*

So off you go on your journey. Let it be filled with bliss, consciousness and unconditional love!

Blessings,

Cha~zay, Ph.D., C.H.

♥O♥O♥O♥O♥O♥O♥O♥O♥O♥O♥O♥O♥O♥O♥O♥O♥O♥O♥O♥O♥O♥O♥O♥O♥O♥O♥O♥O♥O♥O♥

Miscellaneous and Resources

♥○♥

Core Freedom - A Life Skills Community

Core Freedom is Dr. Cha~zay's private community where all members are personally hand-picked by her. This life skills community spans the globe with community members participating from all corners of the world. Core Freedom is a place where people can keep it real! How refreshing to find a place where real people share practical solutions to navigate through life with more fun, love and insights! Here our motto is to serve the evolution of each other's soul. If the evolution of your soul matters to you, you've come to the right place!

A Home Away From Home

At Core Freedom our main focus is to provide a 'home away from home' for all who strive for true freedom, peace and unconditional love at their very core. If kindness and complete acceptance is what you're looking for, you're in the right place. We believe that self mastery, transcendence, transmutation and non-attachment are the answers to all suffering. Add to this practical, down-to-earth, grounded tips on how to make life oh-so-much more delightful, you have the recipe for success!

What We're About

Freedom, peace, hope and unconditional love permeate all areas of life - your personal and professional life as well, and we affect each other as a world community. We are a sacred haven where real people find real answers to all kinds of questions related to life. Here you will find topics related to personal development, spirituality, love, metaphysics. Here we practice our intuitive senses and do dream analysis, we talk about astrology and many

other fun topics. We even have an entire section on how to bring your professional blessing to the world in an authentic way.

Members are Individually Approved

We get thousands of hits every day, in fact, we get over 150 new membership requests per day, almost all of which are gracefully declined. To preserve and uphold the sacredness of our space we carefully screen and individually approve every single member. From time to time we close our forum to new memberships all together to let our family feel the integration of our newest members. We do not experience spam in our community and everyone is protective of the sacred space we have created here. We want to keep it this way. Our moderators and staff members immediately ban members who even remotely as attempt 'funny business.' When you are accepted into this community, this becomes your community and when you become a member you are not just a forum member, you become a family member. All of us here at Core Freedom consider this our 'home away from home.'

Benefits For Joining Our Family

The list of benefits for becoming a family member is ever-growing:

❖ Core Freedom serves as your expanded family, we are your 'home away from home'

❖ Our members enjoy increased confidence and self-esteem

❖ As a member you can enlist your business and service in our directory listing

❖ Use our Marketplace/Classified section to advertise your products, services, books and more

❖ Have the opportunity to become a community leader and build your own forum right within our community (see more below)

❖ Build new and amazing friendships and a private and professional network with like-minded people from all over the world

❖ Expand your knowledge with our eBooks and videos located within our Spiritual Wealth Library and Video Library. Members have access to customized, new, never-before heard-or-seen classes and workshops, products and tele-seminars that will provide you with the spiritual base that may just propel you forward in the direction you've been looking to grow for a long time

Become a Community Leader With Us

Are you interested in mentoring your own community and moderating your own forum? As a Core Freedom Community Leader you can create your own forum.

While our Core Freedom community receives thousands of hits every day, your own forums receive the fruits of our marketing efforts. You are free to do your own marketing and let your current readership know that you are now managing your own forum here at Core Freedom. As a community leader of your own forum you are in charge of moderating your own forum(s). Our staff is responsible for the upkeep of our overall forum and we do monitor for spam. With this membership you are able to accept or reject members into your own community. You can create an open social forum or create a private community.

Cost:

Silver Moon - Free
Golden Sun - **$48** every 6 months*
Community Leader - **$147**/mo*
Monthly Advertising - **$127**/mo*

*prices are subject to change, please check the website.

To read more about our community, visit the following link:

http://corefreedom.com/forums/about_us/

To sign up as a free member or upgraded Golden Sun member, visit the following link:

http://corefreedom.com/

To read more about how to become a Community Leader and run your own forum within our community, visit the following link:

http://corefreedom.com/forums/create-your-own-forum.189/

♥○♥

Teleseminars by Dr. Cha~zay

To find out about Dr. Cha~zay's free and fee-based teleseminars make sure you sign up as a member in her community here:

http://corefreedom.com

Dr. Cha~zay holds frequent teleseminars about various topics related to the evolution of your soul. Here are just a few examples:

- Twin Flame Q&A
- Life Skills
- Personal Development and Self Improvement
- Confidence and Self Esteem
- Achieving Real Intimacy in Non-Sexual Relationships
- Gentle and Graceful Divorce Tips
- Relationships
- And much more

To get on her newsletter and to be kept up to date, register here:

http://corefreedom.com

♥0♥0♥0♥0♥0♥0♥0♥0♥0♥0♥0♥0♥0♥0♥0♥0♥0♥0♥0♥0♥0♥0♥0♥0♥0♥0♥0♥0♥0♥0♥0♥0♥

Other Books by Cha~zay

Quantum Love: Twin Flames - Myth or Reality?

Just what are Twin Flames?

What is Quantum Love and Metaphysics and how does this all tie in with finding the nirvana of supposed true love here on Earth through the reunions of Twin Souls? What are Twin Flames?

Quantum Love is a book that explains this seeming Twin Flame phenomena on a soul level with a heavy dose of left-brain explanations. Find out what happens when you bridge the essence of love, chemistry, entrainment, Cymatics and our chakra system under one roof. Let the scales fall off your eyes and perhaps for the first time truly understand what seems to storming and raging in aching hearts worldwide, on a quantum love level. Get the explanations you've been looking for.

♥O♥O♥O♥O♥O♥O♥O♥O♥O♥O♥O♥O♥O♥O♥O♥O♥O♥O♥O♥O♥O♥O♥O♥O♥O♥O♥O♥O♥O♥

"I just ordered Quantum Love two days ago and I can't stop reading this book and I am actually in tears right now over what I am reading. THANK YOU For writing this book! You are amazing. You are such a blessing to those of us almost there, and reaching for the top. Thank you!" **Jamie**

♥O♥O♥O♥O♥O♥O♥O♥O♥O♥O♥O♥O♥O♥O♥O♥O♥O♥O♥O♥O♥O♥O♥O♥O♥O♥O♥O♥O♥O♥

Quantum Love is a book not only packed with divine Twin Flame relationship stories, you will have the opportunity to write your own Twin Soul relationship story by finishing the amazing unfolding of Michael & Alessia's unfolding.

Over 170 pages of informative, channeled and down to earth information gathered in one place to assist in your own Twin Flame unfolding process.

♥○♥

"I highly recommend Quantum Love for all those who truly desire to fathom the real experiences of Twin Flame reunions. The author gifts the reader with a great service as she challenges myths and reality associated with the truth of Twin Flame relationships. We are reminded of the true purpose of such relationships and that they transcend ego thereby birthing a new paradigm in relationships. Out with the old and in with the new. Dr. Cha~zay offers the reader of Quantum Love an opportunity to create their own Twin Flame story... are you up to the challenge?" **Vesna, Twin Flame Artist**

♥○♥

"I just started reading your book and it is amazing, I am so excited to finally read something responsible that makes sense. The truth should make sense after all. Thank you." **Melinda**

♥○♥

"The twin sole concept is very interesting and a new way to look at your relationship or relationships to come. I found the information about masculine and feminine elements useful as it was a way to think about the world that I had never considered before. Quantum Love uses a variety of historical documents and quotes to emphasize the points being made, all of which are educational and informational. A very powerful book for any person regardless of their spiritual maturity. The conversations between Michael and Alessia were a nice addition and showed how the twin flame connection progressed between the two." **S. Coyne**

♥♡♥

"After reading every book on the topic I must say this is the most thorough and in-depth book on the subject yet. Not only that, but I got so much more than I bargained for. This is a book that not only explains this confusing twin flame relationship thing in depth, it explains in detail as to why these relationships are so rare and yet so powerful. At times a tough read because the author really calls us higher by translating her own channeled messages. An absolute must buy for anyone who is fed up with mediocre relationships and wants to create that divine partnership with a special life partner. Can't recommend highly enough." **April**

Quantum Love is in the process of becoming available as a print book. It is also available on Amazon in Kindle format and on Smashwords for those of you with iPads.

Cost: **$14.14***

To get the book, visit the following link:

http://quantum-love.com

*prices are subject to change, please check the website.

♥O♥O♥O♥O♥O♥O♥O♥O♥O♥O♥O♥O♥O♥O♥O♥O♥O♥O♥O♥O♥O♥O♥O♥O♥O♥O♥O♥O♥O♥O♥O♥O♥

Twin Flame Forum and Dating

Core Freedom features a one-of-a-kind, worldwide Twin Flame forum where we answer all of your questions related to the most amazing, divine relationship of them all - what is know as the twin flame phenomenon.

Let us reveal a little secret to you - the twin flame relationship is real, as real as any relationship appointed by our incomprehensible Great Spirit.

Are you in a relationship that defies all 'generic,' normal relationships?

Is what you are experiencing like nothing else you've ever experienced before?

Are you looking for answers but can't quite find them out there in the big, wide world?

Or perhaps the information you have found so far does not resonate with you?

You've come to the right place.

About Your Twin Flame Hosts

Dr. Cha~zay is the author of *Quantum Love: Divine Relationships - Myth or Reality?* She is a Metaphysician with a Ph.D. in Metaphysical Science and a second Ph.D. in Holistic Life Coaching.

This forum will shortly be led by one of our members, another

Twin Flame author, whom we shall reveal in just a few days. Your new leader and moderator of this beautiful forum is a Psychologist and expert in relationships.

Both of us have met our twin flame energies and are providing you with solid, grounded information that you can use to apply discernment to your own situation. Whether you join our forum or not, one word of caution: Please use your own discernment and wisdom within to let yourself be guided through this often difficult relationship. Please don't ever let anyone give you a list that your relationship needs to meet in order to 'qualify' your relationship to be a twin flame relationship. All relationships are matters of the heart, matters of love. And no list or password will ever confine something so beautiful! Use your own wisdom, your own inner knowing, and your own heart.

To join our life skills and twin flame community visit the following link. Please note that our entry level membership (Silver Moon) is a free membership. The Twin Flame forum is a paid membership, you will need to upgrade to Golden Sun status to participate.

http://corefreedom.com

Cost:

Golden Sun: **$48*** every 6 months

*prices are subject to change, please check the website.

♥O♥O♥O♥O♥O♥O♥O♥O♥O♥O♥O♥O♥O♥O♥O♥O♥O♥O♥O♥O♥O♥O♥O♥O♥O♥O♥O♥O♥O♥O♥O♥O♥O♥O♥O♥O♥O♥

Study-at-Home Courses by Cha~zay

6-Figure Teleseminar Blueprint Intensive

This study-at-home course is for purpose driven and heart centered entrepreneurs.

Are you ready to work from anywhere in the world?
With just your telephone or laptop?

- It's time to live a life that is stress free, especially free of financial worries.
- To live a life where you have plenty of free time to spend with your family and friends.
- Experience the life where you get to have authentic conversations about topics you are passionate and knowledgeable about – all while getting paid a 5 to 6 figure income – just for sharing your knowledge!
- It's time to live a life that is stress free, especially free of financial worries.
- To live a life where you have plenty of free time to spend with your family and friends.
- Experience the life where you get to have authentic conversations about topics you are passionate and knowledgeable about – all while getting paid a 5 to 6 figure income – just for sharing your knowledge!

Does any of this resonate with you?

Your income has reached its ceiling or you are seeing clients face to face and are trading time for dollars. If you are seeing clients

face to face and love what you do but you simply want or need to find a way to supplement your income, you're in the right place.

You want to start your own business and once and for all become your own boss but buying a business or setting up a traditional business simply costs too much money. If you're looking for an easy to set up and low cost or even no cost way of getting your work out into the world, then you're in the right place.

When I became a single mom while at the same time building my company, I was desperate to create a business that would allow me to work from home so I could take my daughter out of public school while focusing on being a stay-home, single mom, all while earning my own, generous 5-6 figure income.

♥O♥O♥O♥O♥O♥O♥O♥O♥O♥O♥O♥O♥O♥O♥O♥O♥O♥O♥O♥O♥O♥O♥O♥O♥O♥O♥O♥O♥O♥O♥O♥

"I have known Cha~zay for a few years and she has been my go-to business consultant on many important issues. Having watched her go from working for someone else to building her own successful business through delivering her service via teleseminars and workshops peaked my interest as I had always wanted to move to Belize or some other warm climate. I learned the strategies of this program by working with her one-on-one and paid a lot more than what this program costs today - and I'm here to tell you that I am surprise she doesn't sell this for at least two or three times the amount. Thanks to these techniques and having created my own worldwide business offering my services via teleseminars, I have been able to move to Saint Lucia where I've been enjoying the warm climate that I've

been longing for all my life (my health has greatly improved too). I highly recommend this program and working with Cha~zay to all those who want to break through the barriers of the illusion that working for someone will bring you riches, especially else while disowning your own purpose in life. Good luck everyone!" **Mark**

♥O♥O♥O♥O♥O♥O♥O♥O♥O♥O♥O♥O♥O♥O♥O♥O♥O♥O♥O♥O♥O♥O♥O♥O♥O♥O♥O♥O♥O♥O♥

My master mind coach suggested that I'd pick up public speaking. But as with most people, public speaking was my all time biggest fear (today it is my biggest joy). In fact, here is a picture of Robert Kiyosaki and me at one of his Rich Dad Poor Dad events.

So yes, teleseminars definitely had a lot to do with me overcoming my biggest fear! Who knows where it will take you!?

Tele-seminars were a safe alternative to public speaking because they allowed me to spread my message from the safety of my home. Tele-seminars were a safe, easy, and a no-cost way of doing just that. And little did I know that by sharing my expertise with the world, tele-seminars would enable me to enjoy over half a million dollars in income within just a few months' time. The best part was that I was able to take my daughter out of school and we would be able to spend every day together all the way through her teenage years! We traveled and took trips to Europe, went to the movies in the middle of the day during the week. We went horse back riding and here we are sailing in the San Francisco Bay.

Every parent and every child should have this opportunity...

THIS is what creating tele-seminars offered me as a single mom!

♥○♥

"I got participated in this live even last year when the shippable product was not available yet, and it has changed my life. I was stuck and hopeless after finding out that I would become a single mom. Money wasn't enough and working long hours already I felt a sense of desperation that I hadn't felt in the my life before. This training gave me hope and rekindled old childhood dreams that I can truly go after my dreams, make them a reality and at the same time be a successful, stay-at-home mom. I have designed and held a few tele-seminars and they have given me so much courage and hope that I am now designing my extended tele-seminars. Thank you for this, thank you for giving me hope when I felt most hopeless! I'm so glad you are putting this here for others to change their lives too." **Wildhoney**

♥○♥

And you deserve the same type of freedom! That's why I have decided to share my knowledge and golden nuggets with you!

This is a shippable product. You will receive a binder with over 170 pages, 7 CDS and 1 DVD with all worksheets.

Cost: $547*

To get this course shipped to your door and to find out more, visit this link:

http://corefreedomseminars.com/course/

*prices are subject to change, please check the website.

♥○♥

Get Unshakeable Confidence and Self Esteem

From Zero Confidence to Building a Multi-Millionaire Dollar Business

Dr. Cha~zay will share with you the secrets of how during her 15+ year career as a Silicon Valley Human Resources Executive she maintained an unheard of low turn-over rate of only 1/2 percent, when industry average was 10-20% – all while keeping her employers out of employment law court for her entire 15+ year career!

"My secret? It all had to do with high confidence!" Dr. Cha~zay

Listen to how she completely re-invented herself time and time again, building and rebuilding her own levels of confidence and self esteem, and how you can do the same.

As a successful, International relationship and business coach, Dr. Cha~zay knows first hand that the number one reason for employees not to leave a dead-end job is because of low confidence. The number one reason for women not to leave their non-beneficial marriages is low confidence in themselves. Similar reasons apply to men and in general, low confidence, especially in self, leaves people running blindly through a miserable life on the hamster wheel of monotony, causing people to slowly sink into depression.

Signs of low confidence:

- Procrastination

- Inability to make decisions and important choices
- Fear of wanting to branch out and start a long-sought-after career or even starting your own business

- Wanting to learn a new language or go live overseas

- Not getting that promotion that seems to slip through our fingers time and time again

- Not getting the date or life partner we want and deserve

- Inability to attract new friends that are filled with integrity.

- And the mother of all 'signs:' Fear of success!

- And so much more…

This course is for you if you are tired of wanting to live the mediocre life and you want to soar to new heights where you'll discover that there are literally no limits to what you can and will achieve.

Cost: $47*

http://cha-zay.com/tele-seminar-get-unshakeable-confidence-and-soaring-self-esteem/

*prices are subject to change, please check the website.

♥O♥O♥O♥O♥O♥O♥O♥O♥O♥O♥O♥O♥O♥O♥O♥O♥O♥O♥O♥O♥O♥O♥O♥O♥O♥O♥O♥O♥O♥O♥

Free Teleseminar Training Course

OVER an hour of free training for creating tele-seminars like a pro!

Come **join me** for this 75 minute free tele-seminar where I will share with you some amazing and proven results that can catapult you forward into the blissful life you are yearning for!

Visit http://corefreedomseminars.com/training/ to get your free course now.

You can also visit Udemy to get an additional free course on how to create your own teleseminars. Visit this link for the Udemy course:

https://www.udemy.com/how-to-create-teleseminars/

♥O♥O♥O♥O♥O♥O♥O♥O♥O♥O♥O♥O♥O♥O♥O♥O♥O♥O♥O♥O♥O♥O♥O♥O♥O♥O♥O♥

Anatomy of a Goal

5 Things You Can Do To Reaching All Of Your Goals

The Magical Formula to Success Goal Setting

This is an in-depth mentorship program, complete with worksheets and guided step-by-step instructions on how to create goals so that they come to pass.

- Live with more confidence
- Live with less stress
- Live knowing you're always in control
- Smile with strength when in the past you may have lost your patience
- Reach your goals and watch your achievements become bigger and bigger
- Feel accomplished
- Become the success you know you already are within – you're just waiting to break through!

CHRONIC THINGS THAT PREVENT YOU FROM REACHING YOUR GOALS

1. Self-Sabotage

- Not setting goals
- Setting too many goals
- Subliminal messages (media)
- Friends (inner circle)

2. People Don't Know What Goals Are Exactly

- People do not understand WHAT goals are exactly and what they are used for (goals, desire, dream, wish – where do each of these start out?)
- Tactical/Strategic goals
- Wishful thinking goals
- Used to having others telling them what to do (the ultimate hamster wheel)

3. Goals Should Always Be Achievable – Why Are Some Achieved While Others Are Not?

A goal that is achievable always has the same anatomy. Just like a body must be balanced with two legs and two arms, your goals must feature a similar type of anatomy in order to stay balanced and come to pass. Let me share with you the exact formula to ensure your success!

FILL-IN WORKSHEETS

You will receive simple fill-in worksheets that make it very easy and your goals definable. Worksheets are attached to the course material and printable from any computer.

WHAT IS THE MAGIC FORMULA?

Each goal has to accomplish and cover the points I have covered before. There is a science, an anatomy of structuring your goal. It takes but a second to fill in the blanks once you get it. But it can take days and weeks of really tweaking each goal to make it so the Universe has no choice but to deliver you your goal!

Law of Attraction would like to bring your highest desire. However, you are a creator and you can self sabotage the formula by the wrong choice of words and by abandoning your goal a few days or weeks into the journey. So your goals also should be fun and left-right brained balanced.

If you want to really learn how to set your goals for the New Year so every single one of them come to pass and you are propelled forward into he new Year feeling confident, then you may want to take our 3 week Goals Anatomy Course. It's a 3 hour Tele-Seminar where I cover every point in detail and give you the fill-in-the-blank worksheets so all of your goals will be reached.

It's not enough to create sassy goals, it's also important to structure them so all of the quadrants of what make you a balanced human being can find happiness and new energy to go after your goals. What I mean is that there needs to be a balance between the right goals, and I'll teach you exactly how to put those quadrants together.

If you want to do this alone, let me now cover the 5 points I promised so you can finish this year with a great new plan for the New and upcoming year, with more confidence that you will undoubtedly achieve your new goals.

SPECIAL 3-WEEK MENTORSHIP – THE ANATOMY OF GOAL SETTING

- 3 classes, step-by-step guidance
- Includes worksheets
- Recorded calls
- Forum Support with other Members
- Download the course modules and participate at your own timing

Cost: **$297***

Visit this link to get your course now:

http://cha-zay.com/new-mentorship-program-anatomy-of-a-goal/

*prices are subject to change, please check the website.

♥O♥O♥O♥O♥O♥O♥O♥O♥O♥O♥O♥O♥O♥O♥O♥O♥O♥O♥O♥O♥O♥O♥O♥O♥O♥O♥O♥O♥O♥O♥O♥O♥

Donations

If you have received this book in eBook format and you have not yet made a donation, would you kindly consider participating in the energy exchange that is so important to retaining our universal balance?

The eBook version of this book is updated and sent out to all who are on the list. To get your newest version make your donation now by going to this link:

http://corefreedom.com/resources/book-im-dying-shit-not-again.8/

We thank you for your integrity and honesty.

♥O♥O♥O♥O♥O♥O♥O♥O♥O♥O♥O♥O♥O♥O♥O♥O♥O♥O♥O♥O♥O♥O♥O♥O♥O♥O♥O♥O♥O♥O♥O♥O♥

Speaking and Appearances

To hire Dr. Cha~zay for your next radio show or to have her appear at your next conference, please contact her office:

Telephone U.S.: 901.800.9696
eMail: media@CoreFreedom.com
Website: www.CoreFreedom.com
Facebook: www.Facebook.com/drchazay
YouTube: www.youtube.com/BlueprintForLove

♥o♥o♥o♥o♥o♥o♥o♥o♥o♥o♥o♥o♥o♥o♥o♥o♥o♥o♥o♥o♥o♥o♥o♥o♥o♥o♥o♥o♥o♥o♥

Resources

Make a **donation** for this book:
https://www.paypal.com/cgi-bin/webscr?cmd=_s-xclick&hosted_button_id=ACUY24EVQJNV6

Dr. Cha~zay's Life Skills **Community**:
http://corefreedom.com

Dr. Cha~zay's personal **Consulting** Site:
http://cha-zay.com

Dr. Cha~zay on **Facebook**:
http://Facebook.com/drchazay

Dr. Cha~zay on **YouTube**:
http://Youtube.com/BlueprintforLove

Dr. Cha~zay's **6-Figure Teleseminar Blueprint Intensive**:
http://corefreedomseminars.com/course/

Dr. Cha~zay's free **Teleseminar Training**:
http://corefreedomseminars.com/training/

Dr. Cha~zay's **Anatomy of a Goal** Course:
http://cha-zay.com/new-mentorship-program-anatomy-of-a-goal/

Book: *Quantum Love: Twin Flames - Myth or Reality?*
http://quantum-love.com

Udemy Courses by Dr. Cha~zay
https://www.udemy.com/how-to-create-teleseminars/

Notes

Made in the USA
Lexington, KY
02 August 2015